QUEEN ELIZABETH
The Queen Mother

QUEEN ELIZABETH
The Queen Mother

Patrick Montague-Smith

British Heritage Press

Dedication

To my wife, Annabelle

Acknowledgments

I am grateful for the gracious permission of Her Majesty The Queen for the republication of material which is subject to copyright. These extracts from the Royal Archives appeared in *King George VI, His Life and Reign*, 1958, by Sir John Wheeler-Bennett, and I also thank the publishers, Macmillan Ltd for allowing me to use them.

I also thank the following publishers and literary agents for allowing me to quote from the following publications: Country Life Books, an imprint of Newnes Books, a division of The Hamlyn Publishing Group Ltd, from *The Country Life Book of Queen Elizabeth The Queen Mother*, 1983, by Godfrey Talbot: Hodder & Stoughton, and David Higham Associates Ltd for American rights, from *Queen Elizabeth the Queen Mother*, 1975, by Dorothy Laird: W. H. Allen & Co, and Rupert Crew Ltd for American rights, from *The Queen Mother Herself*, 1979 by Helen Cathcart; the Rt. Hon. the Earl of Airlie, from *Thatched with Gold, the Memoirs of Mabell, Countess of Airlie*, 1952, edited by Jennifer Ellis: Hutchinson Publishing Group Ltd from *Queen Elizabeth*, 1937, by Lady Cynthia Asquith, and *Elizabeth the Queen Mother*, 1953, by Jennifer Ellis: Collins Publishers, from *The Diaries and Letters of Harold Nicolson*, 1930–39 and 1939–45, edited by Nigel Nicolson: Weidenfeld (Publishers) Ltd., from *Chips – the Diaries of Sir Henry Channon*, 1969, edited by Robert Rhodes James, and *The Nöel Coward Diaries*, 1982, edited by Graham Payn and Sheridan Morley: Robert Hale Ltd, from *Thirty Years a Queen*, 1958, by Geoffrey Wakeford; Michael Joseph Ltd, from *Out on a Wing*, 1968, by Sir Miles Thomas, and A. D. Peters & Co. Ltd, from *Memoirs of Lord Chandos*, 1962.

I would like to thank Lieutenant-Colonel Sir Martin Gilliat for answering my many questions, the Lord Chamberlain's Department, Mr. Charles Kidd, Mr. David Williamson, Miss Audrey Whiting, the Hon. Lady Bowes Lyon, Lady Murless, Mr. Philip Delaney, the London Library, the Public Libraries of Kingston-upon-Thames and Richmond-upon-Thames, Mrs. Jennifer Burge for typing my manuscript, Mrs. Faith Perkins for skilfully handling the picture research, and last but by no means least, my wife Annabelle, for all the help she has given me.

Copyright © The Hamlyn Publishing Group Limited 1985

First English edition published by Deans International Publishing 52–54 Southwark Street, London SE1 1UA A division of The Hamlyn Publishing Group Limited London · New York · Sydney · Toronto

This 1985 edition published by British Heritage Press Distributed by Crown Publishers, Inc.

Library of Congress Cataloging in Publication Data

Montague-Smith, Patrick W.
  The Queen mother

  1. Elizabeth, Queen, consort of George VI, King of Great Britain, 1900–   . 2. Great Britain—Queens—Biography. I. Title.
DA585.A2M66   1985   941.084   84-29253
ISBN 0-517-45801-2 (Crown)

h g f e d c b a

Printed in Spain

Contents

Introduction

Opposite:

The Queen Mother holding her great-grandson Prince Harry at his christening in December 1984 at Windsor.

It is hard to realize that Queen Elizabeth The Queen Mother, 'the Queen Mum' as she is affectionately known in all walks of life, has now reached the age of eighty-five years. The share of royal duties allotted to her would daunt many a person half her age. What is more, she carries out her programme of events, many of which are humdrum, by thoroughly enjoying them and bringing obvious delight to others who take part in them.

The Queen Mother's story has all the elements of a children's fairy tale. A beautiful daughter of a Scottish earl of ancient lineage, living in a romantic castle on the borders of the Highlands... Then, one day a prince, shy and unassuming, comes to ask for her hand in marriage.... At the age of twenty-two, this girl, also shy and unassuming, finds herself in the limelight taking the country by storm, and known everywhere as the 'Smiling Duchess of York'.

Queen Elizabeth has lived through two shattering world wars, losing a brother in the first war, and two nephews and a brother-in-law in the second. Although never expecting to become Queen, she and her husband, then Duke and Duchess of York, were suddenly thrust upon the throne as King George VI and Queen Elizabeth. A brief two and a half years later came the Second World War. When peace finally came she had to endure the tragic illness of her beloved husband who died only six years later.

It is now thirty-three years since Queen Elizabeth became the Queen Mother. Today, three more generations are growing up. The crown is in the capable hands of her elder daughter, Her Majesty Queen Elizabeth II, who says of her, 'She has been the most marvellous mother. Always standing back, and never interfering.'

A special bond exists between the Queen Mother and her grandson the Prince of Wales, who wrote in his foreword to Godfrey Talbot's biography of her, 'She belongs to that priceless brand of human beings whose greatest gift is to enhance life for others through her own effervescent enthusiasm for life.'

The Queen Mother is regarded as being everyone's mother or grandmother. Day-to-day happenings in her life are treated almost as family occasions and a few cheery words to a spectator will be remembered for the rest of his or her life. She possesses that rare gift not only of having an easy manner and natural conversation, but also of showing a real interest in whatever topic is being discussed.

In June 1986 the Queen Mother will have surpassed the record held by her predecessor, Queen Mary, of being our longest-lived queen. It is an achievement almost impossible to believe as we picture her flying about in her helicopters or enjoying herself at the races.

Lady Elizabeth Bowes~Lyon

Elizabeth Bowes-Lyon was born in London on Saturday 4th August 1900, the youngest daughter and ninth child of Lord and Lady Glamis. Lord Glamis was the eldest son and heir of the 13th Earl of Strathmore and Kinghorne, head of one of Scotland's most historic families. She just qualifies as a Victorian, for the old Queen died at Osborne during the following January, when the Edwardian era was ushered in.

As usual, London was empty of society during that August. Nearly everyone in the social world had left for their country estates. As soon as Lady Glamis' health permitted, she and her husband travelled to their early Georgian house of red brick, St. Paul's Walden Bury, in the wilds of leafy Hertfordshire. The birth had been expected at the Bury, as the house is called locally, but events evidently prevented this from happening.

The christening took place in the little twelfth-century parish church of All Saints, St. Paul's Walden, situated up a hill 1.6 kilometres (1 mile) from the house. It is known as St. Paul's Walden because Henry VIII gave the church, formerly belonging to St. Alban's Abbey, to St. Paul's Cathedral. Here on 23rd September the baby received the names of Elizabeth Angela Marguerite, the second name because her father used to call her his 'angel'.

The main seat of the family has been the romantic Castle of Glamis, in the County of Angus, ever since 1372, when Sir John Lyon of Forteviot, known as 'the White Lyon' from his fair hair, married Jean, daughter of Robert II, King of Scots. He was the King's secretary and received Glamis and the Barony of Kinghorne as dowry for his wife.

Although today Glamis Castle possesses the serenity of a French château it had a turbulent history. Shakespeare is said to have set the scene of King Duncan's murder in *Macbeth* at Glamis though this may be only legendary. Better attested is King Malcolm's murder there in 1034. There was a large faded stain of blood on the stone floor, now boarded with oak, in King Malcolm's Room which according to legend came from the King's bleeding body.

Many of the members of the Lyon family met violent deaths. John, 4th Lord Glamis, died of wounds he received in a fray with the Ogilvys. Janet, widow of the 6th Lord and a member of the hated Douglas family, was burned alive as a witch on the Castle Hill of Edinburgh, 'in the prime of her years, and of singular beauty'. As she was consigned to the flames, the sympathetic crowd stood helplessly by. John, 8th Lord Glamis, was shot through the head by Lord Crawford's men. John, the 5th Earl of Strathmore, was killed at the age of nineteen at the Battle of Sheriffmuir in 1715, fighting for the Stuarts. Five years later, his brother Charles, the 6th Earl, was slain in a drunken brawl in Edinburgh.

Glamis is reputed to be the most haunted castle in Scotland. One of their many ghosts is 'Earl Beardie', 4th Earl of Crawford, a fifteenth-century reprobate. In 1486 his host, Lord Glamis, after playing cards with him on a Sunday, then a heinous offence, is reputed to have thrown him down a stone staircase in a quarrel. None the worse, Beardie announced that as no one else would continue to play, he would be partnered by the devil. In the 1870s, Lord Halifax had a nightmare in the Blue Room, and was convinced that Old Beardie had told him that he had been weighed down by irons ever since his death.

There is also a White Lady who flits about the Castle, and there is a Tongueless Woman who stares out of an iron-barred window. The sudden stripping of the bedclothes in a small room which opened into the Queen Mother's Bedroom could be very disconcert-

Above:
*Glamis Castle, the Queen
Mother's historic
childhood home in Angus,
Scotland.*

Left:
*The Drawing Room, or
Great Hall, at Glamis
Castle, with its arched
ceiling dated 1621 and
two gilt lions on each side
of the fireplace.*

ing. Her late sister, Lady Granville, said that the hauntings stopped when the room was converted into a bathroom. One of the castle's doors, however tight shut the night before, was always mysteriously open in the morning – even after wedging a chest of drawers against it. Lord Strathmore had the wall taken down and the door removed.

The most famous of all the ghosts was the Monster of Glamis. Only Lord Strathmore, his heir and his 'factor', or bailiff, were let into the secret which has long been forgotten. In 1684 the 3rd Earl of Kinghorne, who changed his title to Strathmore and Kinghorne, built a secret room with an entrance from the present Charter Room. It was probably there that the Monster lived.

An unconvincing theory, propounded a few years ago, identified the Monster with a son of Thomas Lord Glamis born on 18th October 1821. It was alleged that he did not die at birth, as stated in the Complete Peerage, but was so deformed that he was not expected to live. When a second son, later the 12th Earl of Strathmore, was born in 1832 he was given out to be the son and heir. The monster was said to have lived for many years, hidden from sight in a secret room though there is no proof of this.

Miss E. Gertrude Thomson, the artist, recalled visiting St. Paul's Walden in 1912 to paint the young Lady Elizabeth, who asked if she believed in ghosts. Miss Thomson admitted never having seen one, Elizabeth told her 'If you come to Glamis perhaps you will see *our* ghosts. We have *several*.' (This was announced with a comic little air of proud possession.) ... 'I haven't seen them yet myself, but some day I *may*.' (This was said as if it might be a reward for some special virtue.)

When the 9th Earl of Strathmore in 1767 married Mary Eleanor, only child and heiress of George Bowes of Streatlam Castle, Co. Durham, he had to take her surname of Bowes for his own, though later Earls added Lyon. Elizabeth confided in Miss Thomson that she and her brother David 'couldn't bear' the name of Bowes. 'We never use it ... We are just Elizabeth Lyon and David Lyon.' In the present generation the hyphen has been dropped.

St. Paul's Walden Bury was inherited by Mary Gilbert, George Bowes' wife. To the family, Glamis Castle represented the summer holidays, Streatlam Castle, since demolished, was for occasional visits usually for two weeks in the year but the Bury was *home*.

In addition, Elizabeth's father had a flat in St. James's Place, London, until 1905 when he bought the lease of 20 St. James's Square, a fine Adam house. This belonged to the family until 1920 when they purchased 17 Bruton Street. Years later, in 1975, the Queen Mother discovered that their old house in St. James's Square, which had been converted into offices and was bombed in the war, had been carefully restored by the Distillers' Company. She twice returned there to revive old memories.

Lady Elizabeth's father, Claude George Bowes-Lyon, Lord Glamis, who in 1904 became the 14th Earl of Strathmore and Kinghorne, was a reserved but kindly Scots countryman who did not care overmuch for a smart social life. He knew of the scandals of some of 'the Prince of Wales' set' and was determined that his children should not be drawn into that circle. On his father's death he became Lord Lieutenant of Forfarshire, now Angus, and carried out his duties conscientiously.

Lord Strathmore was an excellent shot and a better than average cricketer. Sometimes he

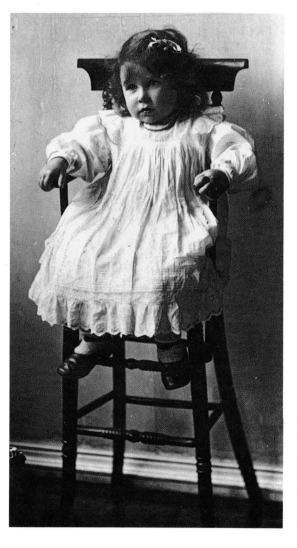

Two-year-old Elizabeth Bowes-Lyon in her high chair.

would come down to breakfast at Glamis practising over-arm bowling with a cricket ball along the passages. When bowling his leg-breaks, he once achieved the hat trick of three wickets in three balls against the Dundee Drapers. To celebrate this his team bought him a much-needed new panama hat. (He was once taken for a gardener by a visiting Australian officer.) Another interest was in Association Football. He was a regular supporter of the football matches of the local team, Forfar Athletic.

It was the Countess of Strathmore, however, who exerted more influence over the children. She was Nina Cecilia Cavendish-Bentinck, known to her family and friends as Celia. Her father was a clergyman, grandson of the 3rd Duke of Portland, who twice became Prime Minister under George III, and had she been a boy, she would have succeeded as Duke. The Bentincks came from Holland and an ancestor, William Bentinck, was made Earl of Portland by his friend King William III, himself a Dutchman. The Bentincks did not like their hyphenated name of Cavendish any more than the Lyons did Bowes. Like the Lyons, they had inherited Royal blood, and Lady Strathmore counted among her forbears, Henry VIII's favourite sister, Mary Tudor, widow of King Louis XII of France, and Katherine, sister of the ill-fated Lady Jane Grey, the nine-days' Queen.

Lady Strathmore was an outstanding character who excelled in the subjects she took up, whether it was painting, music, needlework or gardening. She was a brilliant amateur pianist, playing Bach and Beethoven when she was only eight years old. There are several examples of her embroidery at Glamis. When the Strathmores inherited Glamis she designed the large formal garden herself, which was completed in 1910. This gift for gardening she passed to the Queen Mother and to her youngest son David, later knighted, both of whom were destined to become Presidents of the Royal Horticultural Society.

Lady Strathmore used her hands to describe anything and everything. One story, which her sons never tired of hearing and telling, concerned the activities of a burglar. At a certain point in the dramatic retelling she would pick up an imaginary pistol and fire it, shouting 'bang, bang'. She had a beautiful speaking voice and a capacity for making friends, hearing their confidences and, when asked, giving advice. In so many of these ways her daughter Elizabeth took after

her. Once, when an awkward visitor was expected, her sister Lady Rose suggested, 'Let's ask Elizabeth. She can talk to *anyone*.'

Elizabeth's birth came in time for her eldest living sister Mary's seventeenth birthday. There had been an older girl, Violet Hyacinth, a particularly beautiful child who died of diphtheria at the age of eleven while staying with her grandmother, Mrs. Caroline Scott, at Forbes House on Ham Common in Surrey. Most of the Ham and Petersham villagers attended the funeral, and there was a deep-felt sympathy for the family. There is also a memorial to her in St. Paul's Walden Church.

The Lyon children fell into four distinct groups. First there was Mary and her brother Patrick, who was a year younger. Then came three brothers, John (or Jock), Alec and

Portrait of Elizabeth Bowes-Lyon at the age of six. She already has her famous fringe.

Right:
Elizabeth holding a parasol as a toddler. Her Majesty is still renowned for her parasols.

Below:
The inseparable pair Elizabeth and David sitting in a window at St. Paul's Walden Bury.

Fergus. After them were Rose and Michael. Finally there was Elizabeth, but she was not for long alone in the nursery. Fifteen months later she was joined by David, the baby of the family. He was more like a twin to her and there was always a close bond of friendship between them. Their mother called them 'my two Benjamins', after the biblical story of Jacob's youngest son. To David, his sister was 'Buffy' as his tongue could not get round Elizabeth.

In 1904 when Elizabeth was three years old her grandfather died and they all moved up one place in the family succession. Her father became the 14th Earl, her eldest brother Patrick became Lord Glamis and she herself exchanged the style of 'Honourable' for 'Lady Elizabeth', as the daughter of an Earl. But she was much too young to understand these niceties of social etiquette.

Elizabeth's nurse, twenty-four-year-old Clara Cooper Knight, a farmer's daughter from the nearby village of Whitwell, had been with her since she was a month old. Elizabeth could not manage to call her Clara when she started to speak and settled for 'Alla', a name that stuck for the rest of her life. The pram in which Alla pushed her around the lanes near Walden is now kept in the Hitchin Museum.

Alla, who was accorded the honorary rank of 'Mrs.' Knight as was the custom, remained with Lady Elizabeth until after her eleventh birthday. Then, despite the child's many tears, she left to go to the eldest sister, Lady Elphinstone, who by that time had young children of her own. Many years later, Alla returned to Elizabeth when she was the Duchess of York, as nanny to her two daughters, Princess Elizabeth and Princess Margaret Rose and remained until her death in January 1946 at Sandringham. Elizabeth was by then Queen and she and the Princesses went to her funeral service at St. Paul's Walden.

Her sister Lady Rose's recollection of the Queen Mother as a child is a typical one. It was a grey autumn evening, with winds howling round Glamis Castle, and Lady Strathmore had gone up to her room to dress for dinner. Elizabeth and David went to say goodnight before going to bed. Eight-year-old David suddenly remembered he had left his story book in the Crypt where they had been playing that afternoon, and now he wanted it. As he didn't wish to go back alone to the dimly lit Crypt with its tales of ghosts, he asked his mother to allow him to ring for a

Lady Elizabeth at seven, the age when a fortune-teller predicted that one day she would become Queen.

footman to accompany him. 'Certainly not', answered Lady Strathmore. 'There is nothing to be afraid of. You must go by yourself.'

David manfully left the room to steel himself for the task ahead. Elizabeth slipped out immediately afterwards and placed her hand in his. 'David', she whispered, 'Mother said you were not to ring for someone to go with you but she didn't say you couldn't have *me*.' Hand in hand brother and sister went to brave King Malcolm's ghost.

Needless to say the Strathmore children were not always good. Lady Cynthia Asquith quotes the following written by an old friend of the family. 'Truth compels me to admit that these pairs of brothers and sisters, though devoted to each other, used at times to quarrel furiously using hands and teeth on each other with all their vigour.'

For Elizabeth there was the shredded sheet incident. She took a pair of scissors and cut up her new sheets into long strips. When the enormity of her actions sunk in, she confessed to a horrified house guest. 'Whatever will your mother say when you tell her?' the guest asked. 'Oh, *Elizabeth*', was the reply. And that was precisely all that Lady Strathmore did say, but so reproachfully that her daughter never repeated the deed.

These were isolated incidents. David recalled that 'I can always remember my sister as being the most unselfish person and a most enchanting companion.'

Together these two played games in the gardens and the 'enchanted wood' at the Bury. They had their dogs and tortoises but Elizabeth's favourite pet was her Shetland pony 'Bobs' who used to follow her every-

13

Nine-year-old Lady Elizabeth riding her favourite pony 'Bobs' side-saddle at the Bury.

where, in and out of the house, and even on occasion up and down the stairs. They clubbed together and bought two beautiful Berkshire pigs, 'Lucifer' and 'Emma', but were horrified a few months later when 'Lucifer' was taken to a local show and presented as a prize for a raffle ticket. One of the children's favourite haunts was in what they called 'the flea house', a disused brew-house, to which the only form of approach was a rotten wooden staircase not strong enough to bear an adult's weight. Here they laid in a secret stock of goodies – slabs of chocolate meunier, sweets, oranges, and even

a packet of Woodbines and matches. 'To this blissful retreat,' David said, 'we used, between the ages of five and six, to have recourse whenever it seemed an agreeable plan to escape from our morning lessons.'

In common with most other similar families at the time, Lady Strathmore did not send her daughters to boarding school, but principally had them educated at home by governesses. She herself taught them to read and write and the rudiments of music, dancing and drawing. Both their parents were religious and at the age of about six or seven the children could have written a fairly detailed account of the Bible stories they had learnt at their mother's knee.

When Elizabeth was four and a half years old a dearly loved French governess arrived, Mlle. Lang, afterwards Madame Guèrin, who had many happy memories of her charges. They called her Madé, from Mademoiselle, but after being with them for seven years, to their deep regret she left to get married. Elizabeth and David saved up their nine-pence-a-week pocket money to buy her a spoon for infusing tea as a wedding present 'because you like tea, and once said they didn't make as good tea in France as in England'.

Attached to the parcel was a card, which read: 'To Madé with very best wishes on her marriage from Elizabeth and David. P.S. We hope Edmont [sic] will be kind to you.'

One of Madame Guèrin's recollections has a strangely prophetic quality. At a garden party in aid of some charity there was a gipsy palmist. 'Did you have your hand read?' asked Madé.' Elizabeth, then aged seven, laughed, 'Yes, I did. She says I'm going to be a Queen when I grow up! Isn't it silly.' 'That you can't be unless they change the laws of England for you,' answered Mademoiselle. Elizabeth tossed her hat on a chair. 'Who wants to be a Queen anyway.' She danced round the room singing a French nursery rhyme she had been taught, *'s'il fleurisse je serai reine'* (if it blossoms I shall be Queen).

Another vivid memory with the same essence of prophecy is recalled by Dr. John Stirton, Minister of Glamis, and later Minister at Crathie and Chaplain to the King. He was invited to the Castle to watch young Elizabeth and David perform a graceful minuet, she in a red silk dress of the time of James VI and he attired as the family jester. (The Strathmores were the last family in Scotland to maintain a jester, whose outfit is still kept in the Drawing Room.)

When the music stopped the little dancers made a low bow and curtsey. Dr. Stirton was highly impressed. He asked her whose character she was adopting. She answered

The 'two Benjamins', Elizabeth and David Bowes-Lyon, sitting on an old gun at Glamis Castle.

15

'Princess Elizabeth' and her brother David, as 'the Jester', with their dancing master, Mr. Neal, at Glamis Castle in 1909.

with great *empressement* 'I call myself the Princess Elizabeth'.

There is a charming story, which, if not entirely factual, ought to have been. A children's party given in 1905 at Montagu House in London's Mayfair did not appear to have had any particular significance at the time. It was a typical Edwardian party, with a conjurer and magic lantern. Elizabeth Bowes-Lyon, aged five, was one of the guests. With her cornflower-blue eyes and dark hair, she sat next to a shy boy in an Eton suit, a few years older. She told him about 'Bobs', her little Shetland pony, and 'Bobby' her bullfinch.

After tea he said 'don't go away'.

'I won't, if you want me to stay.'

They remained together in all the games afterwards until her nanny said it was time to leave. 'Goodbye' she said, 'I expect I shall see you again' adding 'what's your name?' 'Bertie' he said. 'And mine's Elizabeth.' Be that as it may, it is reported that neither King George VI nor the Queen Mother remembered the incident.

Lady Strathmore did not believe in keeping her children out of sight in the realm of the nursery and only being produced at a few selected occasions, as was done in so many households. They had the freedom of the house, entered into all conversations and sat with their parents at meals. The piano was usually the focal point of the family and they all joined in the songs, which added to the jollity. 'Life with the Lyons' was certainly not a silent one.

Lady Elizabeth first became a bridesmaid at the age of eight at the wedding of her eldest brother Patrick, Lord Glamis, to Lady Dorothy Osborne, daughter of the Duke of Leeds. She wore a frock of white muslin and lace and carried a bouquet of red roses. Two years later she was a bridesmaid at her sister Mary's wedding to Lord Elphinstone at St. Margaret's, Westminster, this time in a frock based on a picture by Romney. In May 1916 she was a bridesmaid to her sister Lady Rose at her wedding at St. James's Piccadilly to Commander William Leveson-Gower,

Opposite:
A charming water-colour of eight-year-old Lady Elizabeth by Mabel E. Hankey in 1908.

16

Lady Elizabeth Bowes-Lyon at the age of fourteen. The Great War broke out on her birthday, 4th August 1914.

younger brother of Earl Granville to whom he ultimately succeeded.

Sorrow first came to her when her brother Alec died at Glamis in 1911 aged twenty-four. To take her mind off this tragedy, she went to stay with her grandmother, Mrs. Scott, at her Villa Capponi high above Florence. It was all a great adventure for an eleven-year-old girl, who had never been abroad before. She travelled at night on the Rome express and was taken in a pony carriage to Florence to see the galleries, usually by her aunt Violet Bentinck. This was

the first of several visits to the Villa Capponi until the outbreak of war.

For a short time during the absence of Madé in 1908 Elizabeth and David went to a London kindergarten in Marylebone High Street. When David started at his prep school at Broadstairs four years later, Elizabeth had her first taste of loneliness. 'I miss him horribly', she said.

Before the arrival of Fräulein Kuebler who remained until 1914, Elizabeth spent two terms at a London day school, kept by two sisters the Misses Birtwhistle at 30 Sloane

Street. Here she became a close friend of another pupil, Betty Cator, who became one of her bridesmaids and later her sister-in-law. Miss Fräulein, as she was called, got on well with Elizabeth, although David was not so keen, and once took her charge to the Earls Court Exhibition. Elizabeth experienced the thrills of the scenic switchback railway, thoroughly enjoying it and screaming loudly.

She took music lessons with Madame Matilde Verne, who remembered her as having a good ear, and at the end of six months could play at a children's concert. These lessons were continued at Glamis until a few months before her engagement was announced. There were dancing classes by Madame d'Egville who said she was one of her 'most graceful and intelligent pupils'.

The Strathmores were not particularly rich and various economies were practised. Elizabeth's tennis racquet seemed to be full of holes, someone noted, and had obviously been handed down. She and David very occasionally managed to go to a play but in one of the cheaper seats, 'because our pockets never bulged'. Her favourite plays were those by J.M. Barrie, but Shakespeare did not come far behind.

Their greatest delight was to be taken to the Drury Lane pantomime, a most lavish affair, during the Christmas holidays, 'when we were enthralled from start to finish', David said. He added that they 'usually had insufferable headaches from the unaccustomed glare'.

Once, when funds were low, Elizabeth had to appeal by telegram to her father: 'Strathmore, Glamis, Scotland. SOS LSD RSVP. ELIZABETH'. This was successful!

On Saturday 4th August 1914 Lady Elizabeth Bowes-Lyon celebrated her fourteenth birthday. Her family took her to a box at the Coliseum Theatre to watch Charles Hawtrey in a vaudeville show. However, there was excitement unconnected with the theatre in the capital that evening. Everywhere there were scenes of great patriotic fervour which followed an announcement that a state of war existed between the United Kingdom and Germany.

Overnight her tranquil childhood came to an end. Usually the Strathmores spent only the late summer and autumn at Glamis, but henceforward they would be there nearly all the time – and for a good reason. The stately Dining Room was converted into a convalescent home for sixteen wounded soldiers evacuated from the front. The Crypt was turned into a dining room for them and the Library and Billiard Room were also given over for their use.

Lady Elizabeth travelled to Glamis a week after war was declared. The Castle was unusually quiet though that would not be so for long. The familiar sound of the tap of the cricket bat was missing, for her four brothers had joined their regiments for service in the army, three with The Black Watch, and Michael with The Royal Scots. Lady Rose had gone to train as a nurse in London to equip her to take control of the hospital.

Lady Elizabeth's schooling was largely interrupted as she plunged into all the arrangements made for the reception of the soldiers. Chemists were ransacked for every sort of medicine. Tobacco, cigarettes and

Lady Elizabeth and David Bowes-Lyon with their mother, Lady Strathmore, and a pet dog at Glamis Castle.

other comforts were laid in. Socks, scarves and gloves were knitted for estate workers and others who enlisted in the local battalion, The 5th Black Watch. The Billiard Room became piled high with knitted garments, bandages, mufflers, sheepskin coats and other comforts for the soldiers. The first batch of wounded arrived from the Royal Infirmary Dundee in December 1914. All were made to feel thoroughly at home.

One of the Queen Mother's most vivid memories was of the first Christmas of the war. A giant Christmas tree was set up in the Crypt. A circle of men dressed in hospital blue stood round the tree singing Christmas carols by candlelight. The tree was hung with presents for everyone: soldiers, family and staff. Everyone that Christmas hoped that peace would not be far off.

Lady Elizabeth Bowes-Lyon grew up into a self-assured young lady. She was full of fun and not above playing an occasional prank. She once escorted her twelve-year-old brother David around the soldiers' quarters, having first dressed him up as a fashionable young lady visitor with a large hat covering his golden hair. They revealed the plot on the following day. Her sense of fun would sometimes bubble up at unlikely times. Lady Strathmore normally played the harmonium for Sunday services in the chapel at Glamis, and sometimes her daughter deputized. Once

instead of the expected Handel the congregation heard lively variations on the theme of 'Yip I Addy I Ay'. Even Lord Strathmore did not accept her excuse that she could not think of anything else to play!

During September 1914 two of Lord Strathmore's sons married: on the 17th, Fergus to Christian, daughter of the Earl of Portarlington, and on the 29th, John to Fenella, Lord Clinton's daughter. Just a year later, in the middle of September 1915, Fergus was able to get a rushed leave to come home to see his wife and their new daughter. It was a short leave, for on the 20th September he had to return to the front.

The terrible Battle of Loos started three days later. On the following day a telegram was received with the news that Captain Fergus Bowes-Lyon had been killed in action at the taking and holding of the Hohenzollern Redoubt.

The family were grief-stricken but life had to go on. Lady Elizabeth continued to roll bandages, help the injured to write letters home and organize the soldiers' entertainment. Occasionally, if pressed, she would sing some of their favourite songs to them. She was very popular but had to be careful not to let one soldier get more of her time than another. One soldier said that when next he went into action he would wear a label 'please return to Glamis Castle'.

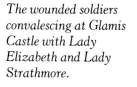

The wounded soldiers convalescing at Glamis Castle with Lady Elizabeth and Lady Strathmore.

The Earl and Countess of Strathmore and their family at tea in the Drawing Room at Glamis. A painting by Alexandro Calani Chili in 1909.

The castle itself might not have been there for anyone to return to had it not been for Lady Elizabeth's vigilance. In December 1916 she noticed that a fire had broken out in one of the upper rooms of the central Keep and immediately rang no less than three local fire brigades for assistance. The Keep is over 27.5m (90ft) high and at that height the wind quickly spread the flames. Elizabeth organized a long queue of some thirty people who passed valuable pictures and furniture from hand to hand until they were carried to safety.

The height of the Keep and the distance from the local river, the Deane, proved to be too great for the hoses of the Glamis and Forfar brigades. The flames were winning the battle when at last the fire engines from Dundee arrived. There were great cheers. Though eventually successful in putting out the fire it was more than ten years before all the damage was repaired.

In the early weeks of 1917 another dreaded telegram came. This time Captain Michael Bowes-Lyon was reported dead. David, at home from Eton, refused to believe the news. He had the Scottish gift of second sight. When an elderly friend criticized him for wearing a coloured tie so soon after his brother's death, David protested. 'Michael is not dead, I have seen him twice. He is in a big house surrounded by fir trees. But I think he is very ill because his head is tied up in a cloth.'

Three months later David was proved right. Michael had been shot through the head during a patrol in no-man's-land and taken prisoner. It was some time before it was known that he lay seriously wounded in a German prison hospital. It was known later that he let another more seriously wounded soldier be repatriated first.

Lord Strathmore invited several officers from Australia and New Zealand to stay at Glamis with him. When, as Duchess of York, Elizabeth visited these countries she recognized several of the men and chatted with them.

There was no stiffness or needless formality in life at Glamis, but ancient customs were

Part of Lady Elizabeth's war work. She was a stall-holder at a 1915 charity sale.

kept up, like having two pipers marching round the table at the close of dinner, with a momentary silence as the sound of the pipes slowly died away.

In autumn 1920 Glamis was the scene of much entertaining, such as a large party given for the Forfar Ball. Lady Elizabeth looked particularly lovely in a rose brocade Vandyck dress with pearls in her hair. Lady Rose and her husband were home on leave from Malta at the time. Mabell, Countess of Airlie, a neighbour and great friend of the

family, remembered dancing an eightsome reel at Glamis when she lost a shoe. Rather than spoil the reel she kicked off the other one and finished the figure in her stockinged feet.

Towards the end of the war Elizabeth was seen more in London, chaperoned either by her mother or her sister Lady Elphinstone, but these were short breaks. The armistice on 11th November 1918 did not mark the end of the convalescent hospital, which remained open until late in 1919. After the last wounded soldiers had signed the visitors' book and departed from Glamis Elizabeth continued to help them find work and assisted their families. Her parents gave her a coming out dance though she had a high temperature for the day. Her friend, the future Lady Buxton, wrote 'Elizabeth Lyon is out now and Cecilia had a dance for her. How many hearts Elizabeth will break.'

Towards the end of April 1919 Lady Elizabeth went to stay at Althorp to be a bridesmaid to her great friend Lady Lavinia Spencer at her marriage to Lord Annaly. The close bond between the Bowes-Lyons and the Spencers of Althorp has lasted until the present time, culminating in the marriage of the Prince of Wales in 1981 to Lady Diana Spencer.

Sometimes Lady Elizabeth drove down to Eton to spend the afternoon with her brother David. On each occasion she would bring with her their favourite Angel Cake. In after years David inherited St. Paul's Walden Bury. He was knighted in 1959, two years before his death, and his widow, Rachel

Spender Clay, whom he married in 1929, still lives there dividing the house with her son and daughter-in-law and their four children.

Lady Elizabeth was an enthusiastic Girl Guide. At the age of twenty-one she was made District Commissioner of the Glamis and Eassie Parish Girl Guides. It so happened that King George V's daughter Princess Mary, later The Princess Royal, was also intensely interested in the Guide Movement. This led to their close friendship and when the Princess married Lord Lascelles in February 1922, Elizabeth was invited to be one of her eight bridesmaids. For the first time her picture figured prominently in the newspapers.

Where Lady Elizabeth first met Prince Albert in adulthood remains uncertain. Understandably, the Queen Mother dislikes some personal matters being known about herself and this is a case in point.

Sir John Wheeler-Bennett, King George VI's official biographer, mentioned that this occurred at a small dance given in the summer of 1920 for young people by Lord

Fellow Girl Guides present Lady Elizabeth with their wedding gift. It was through the Guides that she became a friend and bridesmaid of Princess Mary.

Twenty-two-year-old Lady Elizabeth shortly before her engagement was announced.

Farquhar. On the other hand, author David Duff considers that it was at the Royal Air Force Ball at the Ritz Hotel, also held in that summer, when Bertie, recently created Duke of York, was the guest of honour. His equerry James Stuart (afterwards Viscount Stuart of Findhorn), son of the Earl of Moray, was dancing with her. In the next dance she was dancing with the Prince.

Helen Cathcart has opted for the possibility of their acquaintanceship dating from the spring of the previous year, 'when Prince Albert was assigned to the Air Ministry at Whitehall'. She adds, 'Princess Mary often enlivened Buckingham Palace with gramophone dance sessions in her private apartments, impromptu dansants at which it would have been strange if Elizabeth and the Prince were not occasional partners'.

Mabell, Lady Airlie, said of her at this time: 'She was very unlike the cocktail-drinking chain-smoking girls who came to be regarded as typical of the 1920s. Her radiant vitality and a blending of gaiety, kindness and sincerity made her irresistible to men. One instinctively knew that she was a girl who would find real happiness only in marriage and motherhood.' She was just the sort of bride who would appeal to Bertie and win the King and Queen's approval. Lady Airlie invited Princess Mary to stay at Cortachy Castle, and Bertie came over to Glamis from Balmoral. They played charades and sang around the piano. Bertie was enthralled at the happy family atmosphere he had never known.

In August 1921, the Duke of York paid his second visit to Glamis. He wrote to his mother, 'It is delightful here & Elizabeth is very kind to me. The more I see of her the more I like her.'

Queen Mary, with her daughter Princess Mary, also came over to Glamis that summer, doubtless to look at Lady Elizabeth. Lady Strathmore was then ill, and Lady Elizabeth had taken over her mother's role of hostess, looking after the guests, of which the Castle was almost continuously full. Lady Elizabeth deeply impressed the Queen by her confidence and personality.

The Queen told her lady-in-waiting Lady Airlie that the Prime Minister had indicated that a foreign marriage at that time would not be tolerated by the British public. 'I don't think Bertie will be sorry to hear that', Queen Mary added. 'I have discovered he is very attracted to Lady Elizabeth Bowes-Lyon. He is always talking about her.'

Queen Mary was now convinced that Elizabeth was the only girl who would make Bertie happy, but she said, 'I will say nothing to either of them. Mothers should never meddle in their children's love affairs.' King

Below:
The future Duchess of York with her dog relaxes beside the gun at Glamis in 1923.

George V was also very impressed. When told of Bertie's intention he said, 'You'll be a lucky fellow if she accepts you'.

Relatives on both sides of the family surmised that the long delay in her acceptance was not because of any doubt in her feelings for Bertie but whether she could adapt to the gilded chains of a royal marriage and the constant gaze of the public. Her mother sadly wrote to Lady Airlie, 'I do hope he will find a nice wife who will make him happy. I like him so much and he is a man who will be made or marred by his wife.'

The Queen Mother has denied the story, frequently quoted, that she twice turned down Bertie's offers of marriage before finally accepting. The truth presumably was that he never quite got to the point in these earlier attempts which spread over two years.

In January 1923 twenty-seven-year-old Bertie was asked as a week-end guest at St. Paul's Walden Bury. He must have thought now or never and was determined to propose marriage to the twenty-three-year-old Elizabeth, and duly arrived on Saturday the 13th, no doubt highly nervous as to what her answer would be.

The King and Queen were at Sandringham at this time. Bertie had arranged to send a coded version of Elizabeth's answer to his mother. On that afternoon they went for a walk through the woods. He asked her and to his surprise Elizabeth immediately answered 'yes'. On returning to the house she said, 'I am not sure that I wasn't the most surprised of the two.' Also that afternoon Bertie sent his mother the pre-arranged telegram. It read 'All right. Bertie.'

Bertie travelled to Sandringham to ask his parents for their formal consent two days later, arriving with Greig after tea. Immediately afterwards the following announcment was made in Monday's Court Circular:

YORK COTTAGE, Sandringham,
Monday.

The Duke of York, attended by Wing Commander Louis Greig, has arrived at York Cottage.

It is with the greatest pleasure that the King and Queen announce the betrothal of their beloved son the Duke of York to the Lady Elizabeth Bowes-Lyon, daughter of the Earl and Countess of Strathmore, to which union the King has gladly given his consent.

The formalities were completed with the King's consent, signified under the Great Seal and declared in Council on 16th January, as required by the Royal Marriages Act.

On 20th January 1923 Lady Elizabeth Bowes-Lyon made her first step into the public gaze when she left Liverpool Street Station in a special carriage attached to the 11.50 train for lunch at Sandringham. Here she was formally introduced to the King, Queen and Queen Alexandra.

Sir John Wheeler-Bennett described this as 'an ordeal not to be under-estimated but Lady Elizabeth came through it with flying colours'. Queen Mary, full of enthusiasm, wrote that night, 'Elizabeth is charming, so pretty & engaging & natural. Bertie is supremely happy.'

Less than six months before, the King had written while staying with the Holfords at Westonbirt, 'I hope we shall be as lucky with our daughters-in-law as Lady Holford has been. I must say I dread the idea and always have.' Now he wrote, 'She is pretty and a charming girl, & Bertie is a very lucky fellow.'

A small example of how King George was completely won over was on the question of time-keeping. The King was punctilious in not being kept waiting for a moment, especially by his own family. On one occasion the new Duchess of York apologized for being two minutes late. 'You are not late, my dear', the King told her. 'I think we must have sat down two minutes too early.'

Unlike his bride, Bertie had an unhappy childhood marred by repetitive illnesses, wrongly diagnosed. To begin with he arrived

Opposite:
One of the official engagement photographs of Prince Albert, Duke of York, King George V's second son, and Lady Elizabeth Bowes-Lyon.

Left:
Lady Elizabeth Bowes-Lyon receiving congratulatory telegrams at her London home, 17 Bruton Street, on her engagement to the Duke of York.

*The Duke of York at
Liverpool Street Station
taking his future wife and
her parents to meet the
King and Queen at
Sandringham.*

at York Cottage, Sandringham, on a most inauspicious day, 'Mausoleum Day', 14th December 1895, the 34th anniversary of the Prince Consort's death. Queen Victoria made it obligatory for all members of the Royal Family to attend the annual service in remembrance of her revered husband. Now her grandson's wife, Princess May, later Queen Mary, had the audacity to become a mother on that sacred day!

The baby's grandfather, the Prince of Wales, (five years later to become King Edward VII), thought it would be diplomatic for the child to be called Prince Albert. Accordingly at his christening at Sandringham Church, the infant received the names of Albert Frederick Arthur George, shortened by the family to Bertie. Queen Victoria was

delighted with the first name, even if all members of the Royal Family were not. Princess May's mother, the Duchess of Teck, hoped that George, at the tail end of her grandson's names would 'supplant the less favoured one'. This proved to be prophetic for when he became King in 1936 he reigned as King George VI.

Bertie's father, then the Duke of York, made it clear that he was disappointed; he would have preferred a daughter. His mother, Alexandra, Princess of Wales, sent him a telegram, 'Better luck next time!!!'

Bertie's first nanny was on the verge of a nervous breakdown by the time he was born. The mental state such an illness usually induces means that the sufferer should not be put in the onerous position of caring for young children. However, in this case, it seems that neither the nurse, nor those around her realized the extent of her illness or its effect on her charges. This same nanny often gave Bertie his afternoon bottle feed while on a nursery carriage outing, which was like trying to feed during a rough sea voyage. It may well have been the root cause of Bertie's stomach troubles.

The nanny's condition was eventually reported to Bertie's mother who replaced her with the under-nurse Mrs. Charlotte Bill, Bertie's beloved Lally, an exact counterpart to Elizabeth's Alla.

Bertie proved a shy and highly strung child often prone to tears. There is little wonder, for like his brothers he was often terrified by his father's abrupt quarter-deck manner. 'Now that you are five years old', his father wrote, 'I hope you will always try & be obedient & do at once what you are told', conveniently forgetting his own naughty childhood. Neither did his mother possess any natural rapport with children. Queen Mary appeared to be stiff and unapproachable, a result of being shy. Until they grew up she found it difficult to communicate with them.

The poor boy developed knock knees as his father had done. This was treated with splints, at first worn all night and part of each day. So painful was this that on one ocasion the young Prince pleaded not to have them put on at night. He wept so bitterly that Finch, who was responsible for looking after him, relented and allowed him to sleep without them.

When Sir Francis Laking, the royal physician, heard of this he reported it to the boy's father, now the Prince of Wales, who sent for Finch. 'Look at me', he bellowed, drawing his trousers tight against his legs. 'If that boy grows up to look like this it will be your fault.' At least the splints *did* eventually straighten his legs but Bertie had another and greater affliction, which always remained with him.

At about the age of six, Bertie started to stammer. This most likely arose from being forced to write with his right hand although he was naturally left-handed.

Mabell, Lady Airlie, Queen Mary's lady-in-waiting, recalled that, 'the child to whom I was most drawn was Prince Albert – Bertie – although he was not a boy who made friends easily. Intensely sensitive over his stammer, he was apt to take refuge either in silence – which caused him to be thought moody – or in naughtiness. He was more often in conflict with authority than the rest of his brothers.

'He made his first shy overture to me at Easter 1902 – after I had been only a few weeks in the Household – when he presented me with an Easter card. It was all his own work, and very well done for a child of six – a design of spring flowers and chicks, evidently cut out from a magazine, coloured in crayons, and pasted on cardboard. He was so anxious for me to receive it in time for Easter that he decided to deliver it in person. He waylaid me one morning when I came out of his mother's boudoir, but at the last moment his courage failed him, and thrusting the card into my hand without a word he darted away.

'When I succeeded later in gaining his confidence he talked to me quite normally, without stammering, and then I found that far from being backward he was an intelligent child, with more force of character than anyone suspected in those days.'

Later, his father told Lady Airlie, 'Bertie has more guts than the rest of his brothers put together.'

A painting of Lady Elizabeth by John St. Helier Lander in 1923 at the time of her engagement to the Duke of York.

The future George V, who had spent his early years in the Royal Navy, decided on a corresponding Naval career for his two eldest sons David and Bertie. The younger Prince although dominated by David, studied hard and entered the Royal Naval College, Osborne, on 15th January 1909 as 'Cadet H.R.H. Prince Albert of Wales'.

Although the Prince of Wales ordered that his son be treated the same as any other cadet, he suffered under many disadvantages. He had never played a serious game of cricket or football, he was very nervous, and his stammer was always with him. The routine was rigid. The time allowed for everything from brushing teeth to saying prayers had to be performed at the double. However, perseverance was one of the strong traits in Bertie's character. He wrote bravely to his parents, 'I have quite settled down here'.

He came to make a good impression on his superiors and fellow cadets. According to the Captain of the College, 'he shows the grit and "never-say-I'm-beaten" spirit which is strong in him – it's a grand trait in anybody's character'. Although he found difficulty in making friends, when he did they remained friends for life. One was a young Assistant Medical Officer at the College, Surgeon-Lieutenant Louis Greig, who was to play an important part in his early life.

On 6th May 1910 Bertie's father succeeded to the throne as King George V. Much to his delight in May 1912 he was allowed to accompany the King on his review of the Fleet off Weymouth. Winston Churchill, then First Lord of the Admiralty, greeted the King. This was the first time that Bertie and he were to meet.

The move from Osborne to Dartmouth came after two years. Although his position was sixty-first out of sixty-seven boys, his report read, 'Quite unspoiled and a nice honest clean-minded and excellent mannered boy', to which the Captain of the College added 'I think he will do.' At Dartmouth he learned to row, became quite an expert left-handed tennis player and followed the Britannia Beagles.

Bertie joined H.M.S. Cumberland in January 1913 for his final training as a cadet, when he coaled the furnaces as did everyone else. The cruise took him to Jamaica. There he opened a new wing of the Kingston Yacht Club in somewhat uncomfortable circumstances as some of the girls standing around the platform prodded his ankles and thighs. 'Say, have you touched the Prince?' said one

girl. 'Yes', was the reply, 'three times'. Bertie went on into Canadian waters, which he longed to re-visit, but had to suffer the irritations of being constantly photographed. When he returned to England his father came aboard Cumberland to welcome him back and noticed that he had more self-confidence.

His first appointment as a Midshipman was in September 1913 aboard the battleship H.M.S. Collingwood. Eleven months later, when war broke out in August 1914, he became the only British sovereign since King William IV to have been on active service. He was known to everyone as 'Mr. Johnson'. His father wrote in his diary, 'Please God it may soon be over & that He will protect dear Bertie's life'.

The Prince had only just adjusted to naval life in wartime when, on 23rd August, he succumbed to the first of his gastric illnesses which caused acute suffering. He was moved to a hospital ship, and at Aberdeen was operated on for appendicitis. An ulcer was suspected but not diagnosed. Although Sir Frederick Treves, the King's Surgeon, was strongly of the opinion that Bertie should not go back to sea, with increased pressure the Second Sea Lord relented and allowed him to rejoin Collingwood at Portsmouth in February 1915. 'Went to the Admiralty for the last time,' the joyous Bertie wrote in his diary.

In May 1915 the dreaded symptoms returned and again he was taken to a hospital ship. Still eager not to miss naval action on 'the day', Bertie was able to wring from the King, his Captain and the doctors a promise that if the Fleet put to sea for action he could return to Collingwood.

It was a long illness but in May 1916 he was allowed to return at last to sea duty. Then came the Battle of Jutland. Ironically, although enjoying excellent health for three weeks, he was in the sick-bay when Collingwood put to sea on the night of 30th May. This he put down to suffering from a surfeit of 'soused mackerel' at a hearty supper with a fellow Lieutenant of Invincible.

About 2.00 p.m. on the following day a signal was received that the German Fleet had engaged the British cruisers and the battle was coming in their direction. Bertie went to the turret, and soon the battleship was under heavy attack from torpedo craft.

'I was up there during a lull, when a German ship started firing at us and one salvo straddled us. We at once returned the fire and jumped down the hole at the top of the turret like a shot rabbit!!!' King George V

Family group at Glamis Castle. The Duke of York is standing behind Lady Elizabeth Bowes-Lyon.

gave him the Order of the Garter on his twenty-first birthday that December. 'I feel very proud to have it, and will always try to live up to it', the grateful Prince wrote to his father.

In July Bertie wrote to his father, 'I really think now that I have got over all my inside troubles', but within six weeks he was again struck down with acute pain. His illness was correctly diagnosed this time as a duodenal ulcer. The operation in November 1917 'was very successful' Queen Mary noted in her diary '& they found the cause of the trouble he has been having since 1915'. Although he recovered his health it was the end of his career at sea.

Bertie suggested to his father that he should join the Royal Naval Air Service, pending its amalgamation with the Royal Flying Corps to form the Royal Air Force. 'Papa jumped at the idea', he noted. His friend Louis Greig was seconded to the R.N.A.S. and in February 1918 they reported at Cranwell. Here Bertie saw something of Greig's happy home life. They rode, played tennis and he learned to drive a car.

He became Officer Commanding No. 4 Squadron Boy Wing. No longer was he 'Mr. Johnson' but was known as 'P.A.' (Prince Albert). With his transfer in 1918 to the R.A.F. he longed to get out to France before the final German collapse came, and in October was posted to Sir Hugh (later Lord) Trenchard's Headquarters at Antigny.

After Armistice Day, 1918, Bertie was out of a job, for Trenchard had returned to England. He was entrusted to represent the King at the official re-entry into Brussels.

Determined to fly, Bertie received his wings as a certified pilot in July 1919 when he became a Squadron Leader. So far he was the only member of his family to have become so qualified and neither of his brothers, Prince Henry or Prince George received the official certificate.

Life in peacetime Britain was pleasant. In October 1919 Prince Albert and Prince Henry, later the Duke of Gloucester, became under-graduates for a year at Trinity College, Cambridge. Wing Commander Louis Greig became Bertie's equerry. The Prince bought a motor bike which made his father grumble, 'only cads and bounders rode such things'.

On 3rd June 1920 the King created his second son Prince Albert the Duke of York. This was the historic title that he himself had borne in the reign of his grandmother, Queen Victoria.

'I must write and thank you again ever so very much for having made me Duke of York', he wrote to his father. 'I'm very proud to bear the name you did for many years and I hope I shall live up to it in every way.'

The Duke became interested in welfare problems in the industrial world, and in 1919 was asked to become President of the newly formed Industrial Welfare Society. He agreed, 'so long as there is no damned red carpet treatment'. He visited many factories and went down mines to enable him to learn at first hand the various methods of work. He became known as 'the Industrial Prince', which brought about some ribbing from the Prince of Wales, who called him 'the foreman'.

Discussions led to the formation in 1921 of the Duke of York's Camp. He invited as his guests at a summer camp by the sea, boys from 100 public schools and from 100 industrial firms. Each sent two boys to prevent shyness, between the ages of seventeen and nineteen. Schoolboy and factory hand played, worked and slept together in terms of equality, and entered into various competitive games.

These camps were held annually until 1939, first at New Romney, Kent, and afterwards at Southwold, Suffolk. The Duke of York spent at least one day with them, 'Duke's Day' during which he joined in their activities with gusto, particularly in the camp song, 'Underneath the Spreading Chestnut Tree' with accompanying complicated actions.

The last Camp was held in August 1939 in the grounds of Abergeldie Castle in Deeside. This was to prove very different from the happy carefree spirit which was so much a part of the scheme, for war was just around the corner. In June 1981 the Queen Mother gave a party at Clarence House to mark the Diamond Jubilee of the Duke of York's Camps. She welcomed all those who attended the very first Camp.

Elizabeth standing with her mother Lady Strathmore by the Great Sundial at Glamis. This was erected by Earl Patrick about 1680.

Now that Lady Elizabeth Bowes-Lyon had agreed to marry the Duke of York, no Royal wedding could have been more popular, yet it was not long since the Sovereign would have vetoed marriage to a non-Royal bride. For although she was of ancient noble lineage and had plenty of Royal blood in her veins, she was not a princess. There were several examples of commoner brides for our princes and kings up to and including the Tudors. The uxorious Henry VIII had chosen no less than four out of his six wives from English families – Anne Boleyn, Jane Seymour, Katherine Howard and Katherine Parr. Also, his beautiful sister Mary, widow of the King of France, had married for the second time, Charles Brandon, Duke of Suffolk, a jousting companion of Henry's.

The future James II of the House of Stuart had married Anne Hyde, though she died before he became King. Their two daughters Mary and Anne, both succeeded to the throne. More than 100 years later, George III's two brothers, the Dukes of Gloucester and Cumberland, also chose commoner brides. He did not at all approve of his dissolute brother Cumberland nor of the morals of his wife, Mrs. Anne Horton, and as a result he introduced the Royal Marriages Act in 1772, by which no descendant of George II who was a British subject could marry under the age of twenty-five without receiving the Sovereign's permission. This still applies.

Fortunately, the custom of having to marry into foreign reigning families was swept away by Queen Victoria.

In many ways Queen Victoria was an enlightened monarch. With great sense, she allowed her daughter Princess Louise to marry the Marquess of Lorne, afterwards Duke of Argyll, Chief of the Campbell clan.

When the Queen's eldest son objected to this betrothal she pointed out the dislike felt when British princesses married minor German princes. Lord Melbourne and other statesmen told her 'how wrong it was that alliances with noblemen of high rank and fortune which had always existed formerly and which are perfectly legal, were no longer allowed by the Sovereign'. She added, 'I feel sure that *new* blood will strengthen the Throne *morally* as well as physically'.

Although the Argylls were to have no children, this opened the way for marriages with the nobility. It is evident from Queen Victoria's words that she looked forward to a time when an heir to the throne would marry outside the Royal caste, and this was to happen because of a series of unexpected events.

In the meantime Queen Victoria gave her permission in 1889 for her granddaughter Princess Louise of Wales to marry another Scots peer, the Duke of Fife. Then, in 1919, another granddaughter Princess Patricia of Connaught married the future Admiral Sir Alexander Ramsay but voluntarily gave up her Royal style. Three years later, King George V's only daughter Princess Mary married Viscount Lascelles.

Princess Patricia set a modern precedent by having her marriage celebrated in Westminster Abbey, for strangely enough no Royal nuptials had taken place at this primarily Coronation church since Henry III's son, Crouchback Richard, Earl of Lancaster wedded in 1269 Aveline, daughter of the Earl of Albemarle. There were a few Royal Weddings, however, celebrated in a chapel within the Palace of Westminster, including those of three of England's kings, Richard II, Richard III and Henry VII.

King George and Queen Mary were so impressed with this wedding that they chose the Abbey for the marriage of their daughter Princess Mary. Thus the scene was set for the next Royal wedding, that of His Royal Highness the Duke of York and Lady Elizabeth Bowes-Lyon in Westminster Abbey.

One of Elizabeth's prized wedding presents was one made by a young cripple, George Parkes of Alton in Hampshire, which he presents to her.

The Duchess of York

Just before the Royal Wedding on 26th April 1923, the Press Association issued an inaccurate report that: 'The future style and title of the bride is a matter for the King's decision. Recent times supply no precedent . . . but the Press Association believes that Lady Elizabeth will share her husband's rank and precedence, but until the King's wishes are known, no official information is available.'

For centuries it has been the rule that when a member of the Royal Family marries, his wife automatically carries his royal style. It was not a question of royal favour but of right that Lady Elizabeth became Her Royal Highness the Duchess of York on her marriage.

The matter was corrected three days afterwards by an announcement in the *London Gazette* that the Duchess of York will take 'the title, style or attribute of Royal Highness in accordance with the settled general rule that a wife takes the status of her husband'.

The wedding day started in typical April fashion, dull and rainy, but by 9.30 a.m. the weather had cleared.

At precisely 11.12 the State Landau arrived at the Earl of Strathmore's house in Bruton Street with an escort of four mounted policemen to take the bride and her father to Westminster Abbey. On the pavement a large crowd gathered. In all, there was an estimated million people on the London Streets. This proved to be the greatest assembly of people for a Royal Wedding since the arrival in London of Princess Alexandra of Denmark in 1863, to marry the Prince of Wales, later King Edward VII.

Lady Elizabeth appeared on the arm of her father, the Earl of Strathmore, who looked splendid in his scarlet uniform of a Lord Lieutenant. The radiant bride created a precedent by having a simple wedding dress made, not of the usual elaborate handmade

lace, but of machine-made Nottingham lace which she chose to aid the very depressed Nottingham lace industry. The attached train of *point de Flandres*, was lent by Queen Mary, who also provided the tulle veil. During the procession to the Abbey, the bride happily chatted with her father to keep up his spirits.

At the same time as her procession left, two others moved towards the Abbey, closely

A study of Lady Elizabeth Bowes-Lyon, published in the Wedding Edition of the Illustrated London News, *28th April 1923.*

Opposite:
Her Royal Highness the
Duchess of York, a water-
colour portrait by Savely
Sorine in 1923.

Right:
An official wedding
photograph of the Duke
and Duchess of York with
their parents, King
George and Queen Mary
and the Earl and
Countess of Strathmore.

Below:
The bride leaves 17
Bruton Street, London,
for her wedding to the
Duke of York at
Westminster Abbey.

followed by a third. At 11.07, Queen Alexandra, dressed in violet and gold, accompanied by her sister the Dowager Empress of Russia, left Marlborough House. One minute later came the King and Queen's procession from Buckingham Palace, with their youngest son, Prince George. At 11.13 the bridegroom, the Duke of York, left Buckingham Palace in the full-dress uniform of a Group Captain Royal Air Force, wearing the blue riband of the Garter. With him were his two supporters, his brothers the Prince of Wales in the uniform of the Grenadier Guards, and Prince Henry in that of the Tenth Hussars.

When the bride arrived outside the Abbey at 11.30, with all the bells peeling, she was joined by her two eleven-year-old nieces, Elizabeth, daughter of Lord and Lady Elphinstone, and Cecilia, daughter of Lord and Lady Glamis, who acted as her train bearers, and six senior bridesmaids.

They were Lady Mary Cambridge (now the Dowager Duchess of Beaufort), Lady May Cambridge (now Lady May Abel Smith), Lady Mary Thynne (later Alexander), Miss Betty Cator, who later married Michael Bowes-Lyon, Lady Katherine Hamilton (now Seymour) and Miss Diamond Hardinge. Diamond was a daughter of the

Ambassador to France, Lord Hardinge of Penshurst, a high-spirited girl, who married Captain Abercromby, but died only four years later after a serious operation. Elizabeth received this sad news on board H.M.S. *Renown* in mid-Atlantic.

The bridesmaids were dressed in ivory coloured georgette, trimmed with Nottingham lace, with sashes of green tulle, held at the waist by a silver thistle and a white rose. On their hair they wore a bandeau of silver roses and heather. The Duke of York gave them all a charming carved crystal brooch formed by the White Rose of York, with a diamond centre embodying his bride's and his initials, E and A.

An attempt to broadcast the wedding ceremony failed: the Abbey Chapter vetoed it even though the Dean was agreeable. Apparently they were worried that some people might have listened to solemn moments with their hats on or in taverns! The Abbey was not decorated with flowers. The King had decided at his daughter Princess Mary's wedding that the beauty of the ancient Abbey needed no embellishment and so it was this time.

There were the usual 'wedding mishaps'. The bride left her little white bag containing her handkerchief in the carriage, which was just retrieved in time. (The same thing happened to her daughter, the present Queen, twenty-four years later.) One of the clergy in the bride's procession fainted, causing a delay. Then the two youngest train bearers had some moments of deep anxiety during the signing of the register. They had been warned always to follow the bride but Queen Alexandra carried on a long conversation with Queen Mary on opposite sides of the girls, cutting off their advance. Fortunately, in the nick of time, the two Queens separated.

Among the guests inside the Abbey were many of the famous political and social figures of the time including Bonar Law, the Prime Minister, Lord Curzon, Stanley Baldwin, Winston Churchill, who arrived late, Austen and Neville Chamberlain and Herbert Asquith, who actually smiled at his political rival, David Lloyd George. The most beautiful was undoubtedly Lady Diana Cooper.

The sun burst forth when the bride entered the Abbey, as the King noted in his diary. During the pause caused by the fainting clergyman, when her procession had to be re-formed, the bride quietly left her father's side to place her bouquet of white roses and heather upon the Tomb of the Unknown Warrior. This unplanned and warm-hearted tribute left her empty handed on her long progress through the Abbey.

The service was conducted by Dr. Davidson, the aged Archbishop of Canterbury, once Queen Victoria's Dean of Windsor and Bishop of Winchester. Dr. Lang, then Archbishop of York, preached the sermon: 'You have received from Him at this Altar a new life wherein your separate lives are now, till death, made one. With all our hearts we wish that it may be a happy one. But you cannot resolve that it shall be happy. You can and will resolve that it shall be noble. The warm and generous heart of this people takes you today into itself. Will you not, in response, take that heart, with all its joys and sorrows, into your own?'

To the bride he had a special word. 'And you, dear bride, in your Scottish home, have grown up from childhood among country folk and friendship with them has been your native air.'

Then to them both, the Archbishop concluded: 'It is a great thing that there should be in our midst one family which, regarded by all as in a true sense their own, makes the whole Empire kin and helps to give it the spirit of family life. But above all, it is to yourselves, as simple man and maid, now husband and wife, that our heart turns as you go forth to meet the years that are to come. On behalf of a nation happy in your joy, we bid you Godspeed.'

With the strains of Mendelssohn's Wedding March, the bride and bridegroom, the Duke and Duchess of York, processed the length of the Abbey to be greeted as they emerged by the cheers of the London populace. The Duchess was now fourth lady in the land, taking her place after Queen Mary, Queen Alexandra, who sadly died two years later, and Princess Mary. For the first time she was entitled to curtseys and other royal attributes.

The bride and bridegroom made their progress back to Buckingham Palace in the famous Glass Coach, with an escort of Household Cavalry. Her constant smiles and waves to the cheering spectators gave rise to the hitherto unknown girl from Glamis being invariably styled 'the Smiling Duchess'. Journalists called her that until she became Queen. Even today, on her recent trip to Venice, some Italian newspapers, so dubbed her. From her petite height of five feet two

The entry in the marriage register of Westminster Abbey for the Duke and Duchess of York, 26th April 1923.

Opposite:
The happy bride and bridegroom, the Duke and Duchess of York, after their wedding at Westminster Abbey, 26th April 1923.

Left:
The famous balcony at Buckingham Palace showing the Duke and Duchess of York after their wedding.

inches she was also known as 'the little Duchess'. On arrival the vast crowd thronged the Mall up to the railings. As the procession disappeared through the archway there was a pause while the Royal Party made their way up to the famous balcony. Here they were later joined by the King and Queen, Queen Alexandra and the Duchess's parents. They soon withdrew, leaving the Duke and Duchess to acknowledge the cheers themselves.

There were 123 guests at the Wedding Breakfast. Sixty-six were near relations who sat at the six circular tables in the State Dining Room. The remainder were in the Ball Supper Room. There were eight courses served, including Consommé à la Windsor, Suprêmes de saumon Reine Mary, Côtelettes d'agneau Prince Albert, Chapons à la Strathmore, and Duchess Elizabeth Strawberries. Each table was decorated with pink tulips and white lilac.

The wedding cake of four tiers, made in Edinburgh by McVitie & Price, towered 2.74m (9ft) high and weighed 408kg (800lb). The lowest tier was decorated with their combined coat of arms, the second with the Strathmore arms, the third with the Duke of York's arms, while the top, symbolizing love and peace, was surmounted by a vase of white flowers. In the cake were hidden gold charms, much sought after by the younger guests.

At the wedding reception, Princess Marie Louise remarked to Lady Strathmore, 'how lovely Elizabeth is'. 'Yes', Lady Strathmore answered, 'I have never heard an ugly word pass that child's lips'.

When the bride and bridegroom left in an open landau, drawn by four greys, guests showered them with pink rose petals. The Prince of Wales, managed to hit the bridegroom in the face with a screwed-up packet. For the last time on that momentous day the London crowds cheered them all the way to Waterloo Station.

A special train, driven by Mr. Wiggs, left at 4.35 p.m., to take them to Great Bookham, Surrey. Their destination for the first two weeks of their honeymoon was Polesden Lacey, the lovely regency home of Mrs. Ronnie Greville, the Edwardian hostess, and a friend of both the bride and bridegroom. While there they played golf, walked through the countryside amidst the rolling North Downs, and relaxed in the rose garden.

On 7th May they returned briefly to Bruton Street, and took the train the same night from Euston, bound for Scotland for the remainder of their honeymoon. On arrival at Glamis they found the weather appalling. The Duchess developed whooping cough, 'not a very romantic disease', she later said, and spent most of the time in the suite of rooms, which thereafter were always offered to them when they stayed there.

After their honeymoon they travelled south to Frogmore House in Windsor Home Park, as White Lodge, Richmond Park, given to them by the King, was being modernized.

White Lodge was Queen Mary's idea. She was devoted to the house, which had long been her parents' home. David had been born there, and she supervised its redecoration.

The Duke and Duchess of York asked the King and Queen for luncheon during Ascot week. 'I had better warn you', the Duke wrote to his mother, 'that our cook is not very good, but she can do the plain dishes well, and I know you like that sort.'

The King and Queen were delighted with their visit, but the Yorks never cared for White Lodge. Though only a small house, there were too many corridors, and it was awkward to run and heat. Richmond Park also proved to be too far from London for their many engagements. When the Prince of Wales visited them, he was surprised at the number of mahogany lavatories there, and agreed it was a very *commodious* house. It is now the Royal Ballet School.

The Duchess of York's first public appearance as a member of the Royal Family, was on 30th June 1923, when she and her husband accompanied the King and Queen to the R.A.F. Pageant at Hendon. During

The balcony at Buckingham Palace. The Duke and Duchess of York appear with King George, Queen Mary and Queen Alexandra.

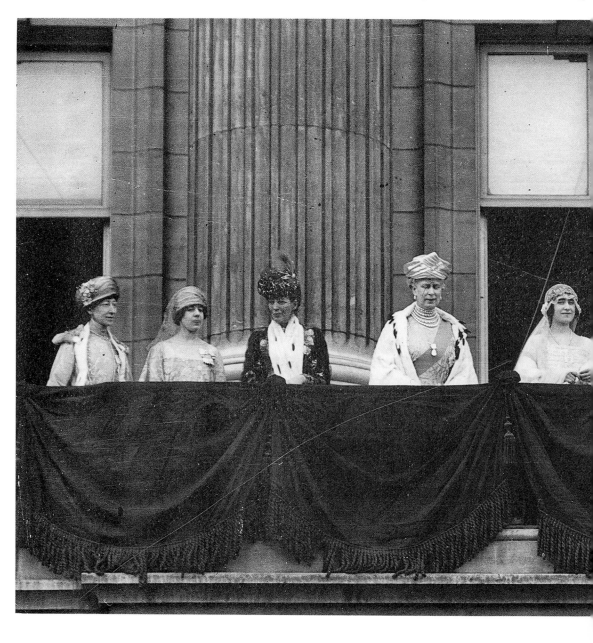

July, they spent a ceremonial week at Holyrood-house in Edinburgh. After centuries of neglect this historic building was restored as a residential palace through Queen Mary's efforts.

During that autumn, the Duke and Duchess spent a few days at Holwick Park, Co. Durham, an estate belonging to Lord Strathmore. While they were there, Lord Curzon, the Foreign Secretary, put pressure on the King to send them to Yugoslavia, not only to act as godparents to the infant Crown Prince (later King) Peter, King Alexander's son and heir, but also to represent the King at the wedding on the following day of Alexander's cousin Prince Paul to Princess Olga.

Bertie was annoyed. 'Curzon should be drowned for giving me such short notice. He must know things are different now', he wrote to his Comptroller, Louis Greig, who was to retire in the following year. Nevertheless, the Duke and Duchess left for Belgrade on 18th October.

The 2.74m (9ft) high wedding cake with four ornamented tiers made by McVitie & Price.

As 'koom' (or godfather), the Duke found he had sole charge of the infant prince, and it was his quick thinking that prevented a tragedy. He had to carry the baby on a cushion for most of the service. When the old and shaking Patriarch of the Serbian Orthodox Church stretched out to receive the baby for total immersion, the child wriggled out of his grasp and disappeared into the font. With a quick movement, the Duke scooped up the baby, which he returned into the Patriarch's shaking hands.

'You can imagine what I felt like carrying the baby on a cushion', the Duke wrote to his father. 'It screamed most of the time which drowned the singing & the service altogether.'

The wedding passed off without incident. Accommodation at King Alexander's new royal palace left something to be desired,

Right:
Goodbyes from
Buckingham Palace as the
Duke and Duchess of
York leave in an open
carriage for their
honeymoon.

however. According to the Duke, 'we were not too comfortable & there was no hot water!!' These occasions were the first meeting between his Duchess and an array of her husband's royal relations abroad. 'They were all enchanted with Elizabeth', her husband wrote home, 'especially Cousin Missy' (Missy was Queen Marie of Romania, daughter of Bertie's great-uncle, Alfred, Duke of Edinburgh). Years later, when Prince Paul was in exile in South Africa, the Queen Mother called to cheer him up.

The British Empire Exhibition was opened by the King on 23rd April 1924, and it was the first time the nation heard him broadcast. With him were the Prince of Wales and the Duke and Duchess of York. On a second less formal visit, the Prince and Duchess sat together in a giant switchback, laughing and gripping the handlebars.

For a time the Duke of York rented a hunting lodge at Guilsborough in Northamptonshire. He rode well and enjoyed going out with the Pytchley. As the Duchess did not hunt, she followed by car.

The Duchess attended her first Court Ball that year, which was given in May for the King and Queen of Romania on their State Visit to Buckingham Palace. This was followed, in the same month, by the State Visit of the King and Queen of Italy, and in July by Ras Tafari, Regent and heir to the Abyssinian throne, who afterwards reigned as Emperor Haile Selassie of the renamed Ethiopia. The Duke of York met him at Victoria Station.

Left:
Bookham in Surrey en
fête for the Duke and
Duchess of York for the
first part of their
honeymoon at Polesden
Lacey, lent by Mrs.
Ronnie Greville.

After Ras Tafari, came a visit to Northern Ireland. Bertie wrote to his father, 'Elizabeth has been marvellous as usual and the people simply love her already. I am very lucky indeed to have her to help me as she knows exactly what to do and say to all the people we meet.'

Also that year the Duchess of York attended her first Court at Buckingham Palace as a member of the Royal Family. She took her place behind the King and Queen on the dais as those to be presented came forward to make their curtseys.

When Princess Christian, Queen Victoria's daughter, died in June 1923, many of her charities passed to the Duchess, including the Princess Christian Nursery Training College, the Young Women's Christian Association, the National Society for the Prevention of Cruelty to Children, and the Royal Hospital and Home for Incurables at Putney.

In the autumn of 1924, the Yorks set out on their first great adventure. This was to be part official trip and part holiday, taking in East Africa and the Sudan. To the Duchess it was her first sight of part of the then great Empire, and her first visit to the continent of Africa – a continent she came to love.

They left London on 1st December, and crossed to Paris and Marseilles, where they embarked in the S.S. *Mulbera*, bound for the Suez Canal, the Red Sea and Kenya. A member of the crew recorded that, 'She bubbled over with happiness all the time. Perhaps her greatest thrill was to cross the

Centre:
The Duke and Duchess
playing golf at Polesden
Lacey during their
honeymoon there.

Opposite:
The newly married
Duchess of York, a formal
photograph showing her
in a tiara and wearing the
Royal Family Order.

Below:
First public engagement of
the Duchess of York at the
Hendon Air Display, seen
here with the Duke in July
1923.

equator for the first time. The Duke and several dozen others had never crossed the line before, so we prepared them for the usual ceremony after leaving Aden. The Duke took his punishment with the rest of them, and you should have heard the little Duchess laughing as one after the other was barbered and tumbled into the ship's pool. We were sorry to say goodbye to the Duke and Duchess when they left us at Mombasa.'

They sat on a special seat at the front of the engine on the rail trip to Nairobi and glimpsed the zebra, ostrich, baboons and wildebeest. After a round of official visits in Kenya, they came to the highlight of their trip, five weeks safari. During this time they enjoyed some success at shooting wild game, and the freedom of nights under canvas, even though at times it involved some physical discomfort. The Duchess wore slacks, a belted bean-shirt and a big felt bush-hat. A typical time-table of a day on safari would have been:

5.15 a.m.	Called.
5.45	Tea and a biscuit.
5.50	Leave camp for morning shoot.
11.00	Return to camp.
11.30	Breakfast? Lunch?
3.30 p.m.	Leave camp for afternoon shoot.
6.30	Return to camp, bath and change.
7.30	Dinner.
9.30	Bed.

The trip produced a wonderful collection of photographs of animal life. They sometimes spent hours getting pictures of the herds, and years later, when their daughters were young, they would look through this collection as a special treat.

Greatly to Bertie's surprise, the colony of Kenya wished to present him with a farm. He was deeply touched by this mark of affection, and referred the matter to his father. Back

came a disappointing reply, 'Of course it was kind of the Governor to have offered you a gift of a farm on behalf of the Colony. I at once consulted the Colonial Office & I entirely agree with them that it would *not* be possible to accept it (as I have telegraphed to you) it would create a precedent, which would mean that other members of the family might be offered farms in other colonies when they visited them. What would you do if the farm didn't pay? The only way would be to buy a farm yr self (& you have no ready money) like David did in Canada & I thought that was a mistake.'

Unfortunately the glorious holiday in Kenya had to be cut short owing to the sudden death of the Governor, Sir Robert Coryndon, on 10th February 1925. Out of respect, the Duke and Duchess cancelled the rest of their safari in Kenya and went immediately to Uganda and then to the Sudan, culminating in a four week cruise down the Nile.

The couple embarked at Port Sudan on board the S.S. *Maloja* on 9th April, and were back in London ten days later, in time to greet the King and Queen back from their Mediterranean cruise. The King had been suffering from influenza and bronchitis, and although now better, his doctors had advised this trip for his health.

Bertie had never felt so fit. He had trekked sometimes fifteen miles a day, and really enjoyed roughing it. It was a question of being happy without any mental stress, a life which suited him down to the ground.

A few months afterwards Princess Alice, Countess of Athlone, on hearing the news that the Duchess was expecting her first child, wrote to Queen Mary, 'Kenya is famous for having that effect on people, I hear'.

For some time the Duke and Duchess lived in borrowed or rented houses. In 1924 Princess Mary and her husband lent them Chesterfield House, at the corner of Curzon Street. Then they leased Curzon House, and in the spring of 1926 they took 40 Grosvenor Square. Eventually the Crown lease of 145 Piccadilly, near Hyde Park Corner, became available. This was to be their home for nine years, but it would not be ready in time for the impending birth.

It was arranged for the birth to take place in her parent's home, 17 Bruton Street, which she had left as a bride three years earlier. In the autumn all her engagements were cancelled. Alla was recruited from Lady Elphin-stone. 'Remember I had her first', the Duchess is said to have reminded her sister.

Sir William Joynson-Hicks, generally known as 'Jix', the Home Secretary, was present at the birth to give witness that the baby was not substituted. (This practice dates from the alleged Warming Pan Plot of 1688, in which, as a baby, the Old Pretender was supposed to have been smuggled into the palace.)

At 2.40 on the morning of 21st April 1926, a Princess was born. It had been a difficult birth and a Caesarean Section was necessary. Nurse Barrie, who had served the Bowes-Lyon family, attended the Duchess, and brought the Duke to see his wife and baby daughter.

A regular flow of messengers bringing flowers, telegrams and good wishes streamed in all that day, making 17 Bruton Street the most important house in London.

In the afternoon King George and Queen Mary drove over from Windsor to see their first grandchild in the male line, who now was third in succession to the throne.

Princess Mary brought an armful of red carnations and chatted to the Duchess. Lady Airlie, another caller, wrote, 'I called at 17, Bruton Street to congratulate Bertie and we found Celia Strathmore there. Saw the baby, who is a little darling with lovely complexion & pretty fair hair.'

Bertie wrote to his mother, 'You don't know what a tremendous joy it is to Elizabeth and me to have our little girl. We always wanted a child to make our happiness complete, & now that it has at last happened, it seems so wonderful & strange. I am so proud of Elizabeth at this moment after all that she has gone through during the last few days, and I am so thankful that everything has happened as it should and so successfully. I do hope that you & Papa are as delighted as we are, to have a grand-daughter, or would you have sooner had another grandson. I know Elizabeth wanted a daughter. May I say I hope you won't spoil her when she gets a bit older.'

Then came the question of names. 'Elizabeth and I have been thinking over names for our little girl & we should like to call her Elizabeth Alexandra Mary', Bertie wrote to his father to obtain his consent, 'I hope you will approve of these names, & I am sure there will be no muddle over two Elizabeths in the family. We are so anxious for her first name to be Elizabeth as it is such a nice name & there has been no one of that

name in your family for a long time. Elizabeth of York sounds so nice too.'

'I have heard from Bertie about the names', the King wrote to his wife. 'He mentions Elizabeth, Alexandra, Mary. I quite approve & will tell him so, he says nothing of Victoria. I hardly think that necessary.' (Queen Victoria had requested that all her female descendants should bear her name.)

The christening took place in the private chapel of Buckingham Palace on 29th May, to which about twenty-five guests had been invited. The silver-gilt font, adorned with cherubs, which was designed by the Prince Consort for his and Queen Victoria's eldest

child, Princess Vicky (later Empress of Germany), was brought from Windsor for the occasion.

The baby Princess wore the traditional christening robe of Honiton lace made for the infant Prince of Wales later King Edward VII. Both the font and the robe have been used for nearly every Royal christening down to Prince Harry's at Christmas 1984. Dr. Cosmo Lang, now Archbishop of Canterbury, christened the Princess with water from the Jordan.

There were six godparents, the King and Queen, Princess Mary, the Duke of Connaught, the Earl of Strathmore and Lady

The Duke and Duchess enjoying the thrills of the aerial railway at the British Empire Exhibition at Wembley in June 1925.

A happy mother. The Duchess of York with her infant daughter Princess Elizabeth, a painting by John St. Helier Lander in 1926.

Elphinstone. The Duke of Connaught was Queen Victoria's third son and a godson of the great Duke of Wellington who was born in 1769. This proved an interesting link, as his brother, Marquess Wellesley, was a great-great-grandfather of the Duchess of York through the Bentincks. The old Duke, turning to Lady Elphinstone, the baby's aunt, said sadly, 'You'll see her grow up. I won't'.

In 1937, 17 Bruton Street, with other houses, was demolished to make way for a large block, Berkeley Square House. Today the ground and first floors of the Bruton Street frontage are occupied by a bank, Lombard North Central Limited. In the entrance hall there is a reminder that 'Here was born on 21 April 1926 the Princess Elizabeth who became Queen Elizabeth II'. There is a also a plaque on the outside, between the two entrance doors, recording the event.

The little Princess Elizabeth Alexandra Mary of York had the same initials as her mother, Elizabeth Angela Marguerite, but as soon as she could speak she called herself Lilibet, a distinctive name, which the Royal Family still call her.

This was a worrying time for the Duke. The General Strike had started only thirteen days after the Princess's birth, but his constitutional position prevented him from offering advice, despite his knowledge of industrial affairs.

During 1926, the Australian Prime Minister, Mr. Stanley Bruce, later Viscount Bruce of Melbourne, asked the King if he would send one of his elder sons to open the new Federal Parliament House in Canberra. This was followed by an invitation from the Governor-General of New Zealand to visit that country. The King asked the Duke and Duchess of York to represent him because as recently as 1920 the Prince of Wales had visited Australia and New Zealand, when he received a delirious 'film-star' welcome.

The Duke of York and even his father had some qualms about his capability in making several important speeches. The Duchess spoke to both the King and Queen, using her influence to show how damaging it would be to pass over him. She was able to persuade Bertie to see one more speech consultant, the brilliant young Australian, Lionel Logue, who had achieved great success with shell-shocked victims in the war.

Bertie had previously consulted no less than nine speech specialists without any success. They all put his stammer down to nervousness so that he was now resigned to a state of acute depression. Then, at 3.00 in the afternoon of 19th April, the Duke stepped into Mr. Logue's consulting rooms in Harley Street. During the two hours they spent together, Mr. Logue pointed out that the stammer was a result of his breathing, and could be cured. It would need all the Duke's concentration, and the Duchess was to play an important part in the resulting treatment.

Together they went daily to see Logue and laughingly tried to overcome his tongue-twisting exercises, such as 'Let's go gathering healthy heather with the gay brigade of grand dragoons'. With the hard work of them both Bertie began to improve quickly. Self-confidence returned as silences were replaced by measured, even if slow, speech.

After a month's treatment, Bertie wrote to his father, 'I have been seeing Logue every day, & I have noticed a great improvement in my talking & also in making speeches which I did this week. I am sure I am going to get quite all right in time, but 24 years of talking in the wrong way cannot be cured in a month. I wish I could have found him before, as now that I know the right way to breathe my fear of talking will vanish.'

In thanking Mr. Logue for all his help, he said, 'I really do think you have given me a real good start in the way of getting over it, & I am sure if I carry on your exercises and instructions that I shall not go back. I am full of confidence for this trip now.'

The Duke and Duchess of York spent a busy autumn preparing for their world tour, and at Christmas they gathered at Sandringham with the rest of the Royal Family. After the death of the Duke's grandmother, Queen Alexandra, in November the previous year, the King and Queen had moved from the cramped York Cottage into 'the big house'.

At Bruton Street the Yorks had their final wrench in parting with their seven-and-a-half month old daughter, Princess Elizabeth. It would have been unheard of to take her with them, as did the Prince and Princess of Wales with Prince William on their 1983 tour of Australia and New Zealand.

The little Princess was left in the immediate care of her faithful nanny, Alla. She spent part of the time with her grandmother, Queen Mary, and part with her other grandmother, Lady Strathmore. The Duchess wrote to her mother-in-law, Queen Mary, 'I felt very much leaving on Thursday and the baby was so sweet playing with the buttons on Bertie's uniform that it quite broke me up'.

During the Royal tour to New Zealand and Australia in H.M.S. Renown in 1927, the Duke and Duchess of York take part in a game of deck quoits.

When the time came to say goodbye, the Duchess clung on to her little daughter for all she was worth. Even after she had handed her over to Alla, she twice came back to kiss her again. When she got into the car to take her to Victoria Station, she was driven twice round Grosvenor Gardens to give her time to become once again 'the Smiling Duchess' that everyone expected.

The Duke and Duchess sailed from Portsmouth in the battle cruiser H.M.S. *Renown*. The original plan was to travel out in an ordinary liner, but for reasons of prestige the naval vessel was substituted.

The voyage out took them by way of Las Palmas and Jamaica, through the Panama Canal, into the Pacific. *Renown* called at Nukuhiva in the Marquesas Islands and at

Suva in Fiji, where the royal party was met by a fleet of war canoes. Here Ratu Seniloli, grandson of Cakobau, the last King of Fiji, who was a cannibal in his youth, presented the Duke and Duchess with a whale's tooth, the traditional symbol of homage.

At dawn on 22nd February 1927 they entered the Bay of Waitemata in heavy rain, and shortly afterwards began their first Royal Visit to New Zealand. The Duke and Duchess received a rousing welcome. Her smile and sparkle spread like wildfire before them.

From Rotorua the Duke wrote to his mother, 'I had to make 3 speeches the first morning. The last one in the Town Hall quite a long one, & I can tell you I was really pleased with the way I made it, as I had perfect confidence in myself & I did not hesitate at all. Logue's teaching is still working well, but of course if I get tired it still worries me.'

The Duchess met several New Zealanders who had convalesced at Glamis. There was Sergeant Bennett of The Black Watch who was with Captain Fergus Bowes-Lyon when he was killed. One young man, who had also been at Glamis, had travelled hundreds of kilometres for a sight of the Duchess, but felt too shy to come forward. She spotted him, and called him over to reminisce. While in the North Island she indulged in her favourite pastime of trout fishing at Lake Taupo, and landed a seven pounder.

Early in their tour of the South Island the Duchess felt ill, though she kept it to herself. When she arrived at the Commercial Hotel in Nelson, she was running a high temperature and had to go straight to her room. She was found to be suffering badly from tonsillitis. After a week she returned to Wellington to recuperate at Government House.

The Duke was dismayed at the thought of continuing the tour on his own. 'It's my wife they want to see, not me', he said. He was proved wrong, for he received a rapturous welcome at Christchurch. At a 'diggers' smoking concert of Returned Veterans, to the consternation of his Household, he climbed the ropes into the boxing ring to give an impromptu speech that brought the house down.

After the Duchess's recovery she rejoined H.M.S. *Renown*, which went on to collect Bertie from the southernmost tip at Invercargill in really blustery weather. They sailed for Australia where their visit began on 26th March.

In Australia they received a great if informal welcome. The visit to Sydney opened 'with a veritable ride of triumph', according to Mr. Ian Lucas. 'The Duke wore the uniform of a naval post-captain, with cocked hat, while the Duchess was looking lovelier than ever in a pretty dress of pink georgette with a flowing cloak, of which the collar was

In their ceremonial cloaks the Duke and Duchess are greeted by a group of Maori dancers at Rotorua in New Zealand.

trimmed with ostrich feathers. Despite the hot sun they rode in an open car so that all might see them.' At Sydney University she made her one speech of the tour. It was short but made a good impression.

They were in Melbourne on Anzac Day, 25th April, where there was a service to remember those who had fallen in the war. Among those who paraded were twenty-nine holders of the Victoria Cross. The Duchess dressed entirely in black, stood beside her husband who made a moving speech after the parade 'That great feat of arms and the heroic deeds of all who shared in it will be remembered so long as the Empire lasts.'

At the State Ball in Melbourne her first dance was with the Governor-General, Viscount Stonehaven, and her second with the Prime Minister, Mr. Bruce. the third was with an unknown man. He was a young Tasmanian engineer who had fought at Gallipoli with Anzac forces and recuperated from his wounds at Glamis. He wrote to the Duchess, but did not think anything would come of it. Then a telephone message from Government House summoned him to visit her on the following day. After gossiping together she asked him to come to the ball and meet the Duke of York.

Dame Nellie Melba sang the first verse of the National Anthem at the opening of the new Federal Parliament in Canberra. There was a crowd of some 50,000 outside, watching as the Duke opened the door of the building with a golden key. He gave them a short unexpected speech. 'I have never heard him speak better', said one Australian.

When the Duke opened Parliament some of his nervousness overtook him and hesitation returned, but soon passed. When the ceremony was over they were very relieved. 'Those happy young people were like children let out of school', commented one Australian Minister.

A very rough buffeting in the Great Australian Bight, on their way to Western Australia, flung furniture about and flooded decks. Fortunately both the Duke and Duchess were unaffected by sea sickness. One of her ladies-in-waiting later said 'I have never known her upset by a train, a car, a boat or an aeroplane. She is impervious. One can hardly imagine a more useful quality for royalty.' With all the State capitals visited, H.M.S. Renown's voyage home started from Fremantle on Monday 23rd May. On board were 30,480kg (30tn) of gifts, including several presents for the young princess.

Three days after sailing, while at luncheon, a serious fire broke out. Plans were made to abandon ship if necessary. While the Duke of York went to encourage the fire-fighters, the Duchess showed no signs of anything being amiss. At last, at about 10.00 p.m., the fire was out.

A few days later the Captain said to her, 'Did you ever realize, Ma'am that at one time it was pretty bad?' 'Yes, I did', she said. 'Every hour someone came and told me that it was nothing to worry about, so I knew there was real trouble.'

Renown's route took the Duke and Duchess back through the Suez Canal to Malta, where they picnicked with Lord Louis Mountbatten, and on to Gibraltar. On the morning of 27th June, the Duke's three brothers came to greet them at Portsmouth. Old King George came to Victoria Station, having previously forwarded instructions for his thirty-year-old son, 'When you kiss Mama take yr. hat off.'

Both the Duke and Duchess were longing to see their little daughter, Princess Elizabeth. It was planned that their reunion with her would take place at 145 Piccadilly, where the Princess and Alla had moved to a few days earlier. Queen Mary, as a surprise, brought the 'bambino' as she termed her, to Buckingham Palace as the Royal party would be returning there from the station.

The Duchess could only wonder if her fourteen-months-old daughter would remember her. Momentarily, Lilibet fixed her mother with an enquiring stare. Suddenly, with a broad smile of welcome, she outstretched her arms. Long afterwards, the Duchess told her daughter how much this recognition pleased her. Princess Elizabeth also remembered when she became a mother. Every night, when Prince Philip was in Malta, she took Prince Charles up to his father's photograph to say 'Goodnight, Papa', before going to bed. 'I don't want him to forget his father', she said.

The King rewarded the Duchess for her great part in making the visit such a success, by creating her a Dame Grand Cross of the Order of the British Empire. She was also appointed Colonel-in-Chief of her first regiment, The King's Own Yorkshire Light Infantry.

Behind the black double doors of 145 Piccadilly, the Duke and Duchess of York settled down to a life of domestic bliss. With exquisite taste they converted this rather austere house into a comfortable home. French windows opened on to the private

The Duke and Duchess of York in their uniforms of Boy Scout and Girl Guide being welcomed at Adelaide in South Australia. She rarely appears in uniform.

grounds at the rear, Hamilton Gardens, with its small lake, where mallards nested, and from here a gate led into Hyde Park.

The Duke and Duchess did not entertain formally on a great scale. Most of their functions were connected with organizations with which they were involved. For instance, Officers of The King's Own Yorkshire Light Infantry and their wives were invited to an annual tea party.

In January 1928 the Duke and Duchess were invited by the National Association of Street Traders to the Costermongers' Annual Ball. This was held in Finsbury Town Hall, and most of the guests arrived in fancy dress or pearly costumes. A cordon of pearly kings kept a way open to the dais, and the Duchess was 'crowned' with a paper hat.

They took part in a set of lancers, and on returning to the stage a pearly doll was presented to her for Princess Elizabeth. They also danced a foxtrot, and after the fancy dress parade, she presented the prizes.

The Duchess has always taken a great interest in the St. Marylebone Housing Association, since it was founded in 1927 by a few friends. They demolished some squalid buildings in Lisson Grove in order to build some decent houses. Then on 9th June 1928 the Duchess came to lay the foundation stone of the first block of flats. Lady Cynthia Asquith quotes a letter from a lady whose home was visited.

'On the wall was a photo of my son Thomas, killed at the Battle of the Somme. Only twenty he was. The Duchess looked at the photo. "How lovely", she said. "He belonged to the Royal Fusiliers, I see", and then, turning away her pretty head, she whispered, "God bless him". There was tears in her eyes, and I felt I could have hugged and kissed her, but I was so overcome. I had to turn away not to break down sobbing.'

In these personal little encounters the Queen Mother is unrivalled.

During that November King George V became very ill. The Prince of Wales, then in East Africa, was urgently sent for as there was cause for anxiety. In one of the Duke of York's letters to him, there was a lighter touch, 'There is a lovely story going about which emanated from the East End, that the reason of your rushing home is that in the event of anything happening to Papa I am going to bag the Throne in your absence!!!! Just like the Middle Ages!'

On 1st December a bulletin was issued that the strain was beginning to effect the King's heart. On the 11th, the day the Prince of Wales returned to London, Lord Dawson of Penn operated to save the King's life by removing a rib and draining the infected lung. Although the King did not die, he never fully regained his strength. In February he went to convalesce at Craigweil House near Bognor in Sussex, and early in March it was the Duchess of York's idea to bring his little granddaughter, Lilibet, to Bognor. The strong bond of affection between King and Princess was further cemented. Another operation was necessary in July.

In March 1929 the royal couple attended the wedding in Oslo of Prince Olav (now King) of Norway to Princess Marthe of Sweden. A journalist there recalled her little fringe, her intense blue eyes and her friendly smile.

On 20th May there was an important occasion in Scotland. The Duke of York had been appointed High Commissioner of the General Assembly of the Church of Scotland. He was the first member of the Royal Family to act since the appointment in 1679 of the Duke of York, later James II. That year marked the end of a long feud, for the established Church was once more united to the United Free Church, 'the wee Free'.

Edinburgh was en fête for a ceremonial week. It was then said that, 'the association of the King's son and the little Duchess, who had become the darling of the people, transferred the routine welcome into rapture'. The Lord Provost presented the Duke with the keys of the city, which in addition was celebrating the 600th anniversary of King Robert the Bruce's first charter.

The Duchess missed the wedding of the Crown Prince of Italy because she had bronchitis. When her husband returned home she told him that she was pregnant, to his great delight.

Every summer the Yorks stayed at Glamis Castle, and there they went in August 1930. Here the birth of a second daughter, Princess Margaret, took place on the 21st, not in their own suite but in Lady Strathmore's own pleasant bedroom. It was the first royal birth to take place in Scotland since that of Charles I's brother, Prince Robert, in 1602.

It had been arranged that the Home Secretary, Mr. J.R. Clynes, whose presence was necessary at the birth, should stay at Airlie Castle with the Countess of Airlie. As the child was expected between the 6th and 12th August, he and Mr. Boyd, the Ceremonial Secretary at the Home Office, arrived on

On the Duke and Duchess's return to London in 1927 they receive the Freedom of the City.

the morning of the 5th. On the 10th at Glamis they met Sir Henry Simpson, the Royal accoucheur, who told them that the birth could not be later than the 11th. They sat up all that night, sustained by constant cups of coffee, but no news.

By the morning of the 21st, in a state of panic, they rang Glamis, with no result. That evening, just as Lady Airlie was dressing for dinner the telephone rang in her bedroom from Glamis. She heard Mr. Boyd in an agitated state, shouting 'I can't go downstairs. I can't find my suit'. He was invited in to her room to use the telephone, wearing his dressing gown, a dark blue kimono. 'What, in an hour', he said in reply to the message, 'You haven't given us much time. We must start at once.'

While they dressed, the cook cut them a few sandwiches. But all was well. They arrived at Glamis with half an hour to spare, and that night caught the train to London, duty done.

The bells peeled. After a day's delay through heavy rain a great bonfire was lit on top of Hunter's Hill to celebrate the royal arrival. Watching from a high window in the castle was the new Princess's four-and-a-half year old sister, Princess Elizabeth.

The Duchess of York wrote to Queen Mary about names for the Princess. 'I am very anxious to call her Ann Margaret as I think Ann of York sounds pretty, & Elizabeth and Ann go so well together. I wonder what you think? Lots of people have suggested Margaret, but it has no family links really on either side.'

This choice did not please the King. The Duchess wrote again, 'Bertie & I have decided now to call our little daughter "Margaret

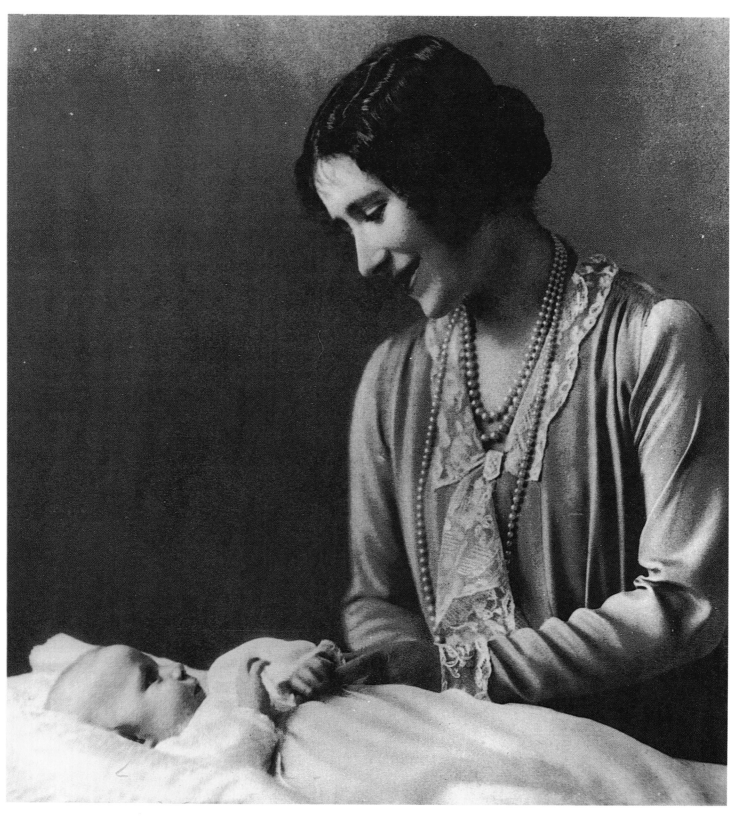

The Duchess of York with her second child, Princess Margaret Rose, who was born at Glamis Castle on 21st August 1930, the first Royal birth in Scotland since 1602.

Rose" instead of M.Ann, as Papa does not like "Ann" – I hope that you like it. I think that it is very pretty together'.

Princess Margaret Rose was christened on 30th October by the Archbishop of Canterbury at Buckingham Palace in the same robe and at the same font as were used by her sister. She was always known by both names in her childhood. She received the second name after her godmother, Lady Rose Leveson-Gower. The other godparents were the

Prince of Wales, Princess Victoria, Princess Ingrid of Sweden and the Hon. David Bowes-Lyon.

Alla was assisted by an under-nanny, Margaret Macdonald, coming from Black Isle in Inverness on a recommendation from Lady Linlithgow. As there was already a Mrs. Macdonald (a cook named 'Golly' by Princess Elizabeth from her mop of hair), Margaret Macdonald was named 'Bobo' by the Princess because this was what she used to call out while playing hide-and-seek behind the bushes in Hamilton Gardens.

When Princess Margaret arrived, Bobo's younger sister Robina (known as Ruby), came as under-nanny to Alla, who took over the new baby. Bobo, the same age as the Queen Mother, shared the room with the Princess throughout her childhood and has long been the confidante and dresser of the present Queen. Her sister Ruby was for a long time dresser to Princess Margaret.

In 1931, Lady Fetherstonhaugh, widow of the King's Racing Manager, vacated Royal Lodge in Windsor Great Park to take on the appointment of Stud Manager at Sandringham. Bertie quickly put a request to his father for the Lodge, which was granted. A country retreat at Windsor was just what he wanted. This corresponded to Fort Belvedere, a short distance away, which had been given a few months earlier to the Prince of Wales, and was his favourite home.

Royal Lodge was then very delapidated. The house had been erected on the site of the Prince Regent's celebrated *cottage orné*, built by Nash, and earlier was the Lower Lodge of Thomas Sandby, Deputy Ranger of Windsor Great Park, who laid out Virginia Water. The Queen Mother has several water-colours by the celebrated artist Paul Sandby who also lived at Lower Lodge. Included is a delightful one, dated 1798, showing members of his family standing in front of this house.

Wyatville's Saloon, the best room in the house, had been divided to make three rooms. This was now restored to its original state and to compensate for the loss of rooms a new ground floor wing was built to the east of the Octagon Room, built by Queen Adelaide. Nursery and guest additions and a servants' wing over an extended garage were added later.

Much work needed to be done in clearing the grounds and planting a garden. A former Deputy Ranger said 'the gardens are the inspiration and work of the Duke and Duchess of York themselves. They were so close together that they always thought alike.'

The Yorks moved into Royal Lodge in the Autumn of 1932. From that time onwards

The Duchess of York inspects nurses when she and the Duke opened the Stuart Memorial Extension of the Harrow and Wealdstone Hospital in May 1931.

they were constantly there, particularly at week-ends. It also became the second home of others in the Royal Family, notably the Duke's three brothers. The Prince of Wales used to come over from the Fort. All three brothers envied Bertie's happy married life. The next to marry was George, Duke of Kent in 1934 to Princess Marina of Greece, they used to come over from their home, Coppins, at nearby Iver. In 1935, Prince Henry, Duke of Gloucester married Lady Alice Montagu-Douglas-Scott, daughter of the Duke of Buccleuch.

For Princess Elizabeth's sixth birthday the people of Wales presented her with a reproduction of a traditional Welsh thatched cottage, reduced to two-fifths of the ordinary size – *Y Bwthyn Bach* (The Little House). This has proved a great favourite with all Royal children ever since.

Both the Duke and Duchess of York liked dogs. In King George V's time, only gun dogs were kept at Sandringham and Balmoral, for Queen Mary did not like house dogs, and there were none at Buckingham Palace. In 1933, Princess Elizabeth, envious of a friend's Pembroke corgi puppy, persuaded her mother to get one too. They chose a puppy, whom they called 'Dookie', who proved to be rather ferocious. More than one member of the household suffered from his bites! Another corgi 'Jane' was later added. They proved merely to be the beginning of a favourite breed. There were other dogs, too, such as the Duke's dog 'Mimsy', a golden labrador, and the Duchess's 'Choo Choo', a Tibetan lion dog. During the war, 'Choo Choo', old by then, was evacuated to St. Paul's Walden. He nevertheless managed to greet his mistress with uncontrollable delight on her visits.

King George V's Silver Jubilee on 6th May 1935 emanated from an idea of his Ministers, but its unexpected warmth greatly pleased him. 'The greatest number of people in the streets that I have ever seen in my life', he said. 'They must really like me for myself.' The King told Dr. Matthews, the Dean of St. Paul's, where the thanksgiving service was held, that it was 'a wonderful service. The

The Duchess of York and Princess Helena Victoria admire an embroidered evening shawl at the Royal School of Needlework's Christmas Sale in London, 1931.

King George and Queen Mary with the Duchess of York and the two Princesses outside Y Bwthyn Bach *at Royal Lodge, Windsor in 1933.*

Queen and I are most grateful. Just one thing wrong with it – too many parsons getting in the way. I didn't know there were so many damn parsons in England. It was worse than a levee.'

To the British public it had almost become a foregone conclusion that the Prince of Wales would not marry, and that the Duke of York or Princess Elizabeth would eventually succeed. Sir John Wheeler-Bennett stated that the cry rang out above the cheers as the Yorks' carriage passed in procession from the Palace, 'There goes the hope of England'.

Soon after the Jubilee, the King's health deteriorated. He fell asleep in the daytime

and even at meals. The final blow to him came three weeks before Christmas, the death of his favourite sister, Princess Victoria. The King used to telephone her daily. He could not face the Opening of Parliament that day, and cancelled the ceremony.

At Sandringham on the morning of 20th January 1936, a Privy Council was held. The dying King sat propped up in a chair in his bedroom, just visible to the Privy Counsellors through the open door, Lord Dawson could get him to say 'Approved', but not to sign his name which distressed him. Instead he made two little crosses. That evening the B.B.C. constantly reported 'the King's life is moving peacefully towards its close'. He died at 11.55 p.m.

When the King's body was taken in procession through the London streets to lie in State at Westminster Hall, the Maltese Cross containing a great sapphire set on top of the Imperial State Crown, fell from the gun carriage into the gutter. Although the cross was retrieved by the Company Sergeant-Major, the new King noticed the circumstance. 'A most terrible omen', wrote Harold Nicolson in his diary.

At King George V's funeral at St. George's Chapel, Windsor, the Duchess of York's lady-in-waiting, Lady Helen Graham, said of the solitary figure of his son the new King, 'I feel so sorry for him. *He* is not going home to a wife behind the teapot and a warm fire, with his children making toast for him.'

The relationship between King George V and the Duchess of York had been strong. 'I miss him dreadfully', she wrote to his doctor, Lord Dawson, 'unlike his own children I was never afraid of him, and in all the twelve years of having me as daughter-in-law he never spoke one unkind or abrupt word to me, and was always ready to listen and give advice on one's own silly little affairs. He was

The Duchess of York opens the Exhibition of Modern Indian Art at the New Burlington Galleries in London, accompanied by the Maharaj Kumari of Burdwan, December 1934.

so kind, and *dependable*! And when he was in the mood, he could be deliciously funny too!'

The Duke of York was now heir presumptive to the throne. He was promoted to the ranks of Vice-Admiral, Lieutenant-General and Air Marshal. His and the Duchess's names now appeared in Royal Toasts, and they were prayed for by name in churches. However, as a family they saw much less of David, now King Edward VIII.

As this book is about the Queen Mother, I will only refer briefly to the abdication of King Edward VIII in so far as it affected her and her husband. As Prince of Wales he had been introduced in 1930 to the Baltimore-born Mrs. Wallis Simpson by Thelma Lady

A miner shows the Duchess of York his Davy lamp at the Abercynon Colliery, South Wales, in June 1933.

Furness, a fellow American. She had first married a naval lieutenant, Earle Spencer, but this ended in divorce. Then in 1928, she married secondly, Ernest Simpson an American-born British subject, a shipbroker who had served as a Lieutenant in The Coldstream Guards during the Great War.

In 1935 the Simpsons' marriage broke up and the Prince's long-standing affair with Mrs. Simpson caused great anxiety to King George V and Queen Mary. Lady Airlie recorded a conversation with Lady Algernon Gordon-Lennox who told her that 'a few months before his death, King George had said passionately, "I pray to God that my eldest son will never marry and have chil-

dren, and that nothing will come between Bertie and Lilibet and the throne". '

1936 progressed steadily towards a constitutional crisis. In May, Sir Henry 'Chips' Channon wrote, 'It appears that the King is Mrs. Simpson's absolute slave'. On 27th October at Ipswich, Mrs. Simpson obtained her decree nisi from her husband.

On 16th November King Edward broke the news about his intended marriage with Mrs. Simpson to Stanley Baldwin, the Prime Minister, whom he summoned to Buckingham Palace. He said, 'I intend to marry Mrs. Simpson as soon as she is free to marry'. If the Government opposed him, he was prepared to go. It was extremely doubtful that

the people of Britain and the Empire would accept a lady with two living ex-husbands for their Queen.

Later that day he told Queen Mary of his intention and on the next day informed the Duke of York, and afterwards his two younger brothers. 'Bertie was so much taken aback by the news', the Duke of Windsor later wrote, 'that in his shy way he could not bring himself to express his innermost feelings at the time. This, after all, was not surprising, for next to myself, Bertie had most at stake.'

By 25th November, the Duke of York could write to Sir Godfrey Thomas the King's Assistant Private Secretary as follows:

'If the worst happens and I have to take over, you can be assured that I will do my best to clear up the inevitable mess, if the whole fabric does not crumble under the shock and strain of it all.'

News of the constitutional crisis had been censored by the British Press, but for how much longer could the secret be kept?

On 1st December, Dr. Alfred Blunt, Bishop of Bradford, started his diocesan conference with some mild criticism of 'the King's unawareness of the need for God's grace'. He was looking ahead to the Coronation, fixed for 12th May.

The next day the London press was filled with the burning of the Crystal Palace. Dr.

Blunt's words went unnoticed, but not so among the papers in the north of England. *The Yorkshire Post* featured the Bishop's remarks in a leader. On the 3rd the floodgates were open. Yet Bishop Blunt had never heard of Mrs. Simpson! He was referring to the King's lack of regular church-going.

The Duke and Duchess of York returned from Edinburgh on the same day, where he had been installed as Grand Master Mason. 'At Euston I was both surprised & horrified', he wrote in his diary, 'to see that the posters of the Daily Press had the following as their headlines in block letters, "the King's Marriage".'

That evening the Duke saw Queen Mary, and his brother, the King. The Duke's diary records what can only be described as his brother's callous disregard for his heir: 'When David left after making this dreadful announcement to his mother, he told me to come & see him at the Fort the next morning [Friday, 4th December].

'I rang him up, but he would not see me, & put me off till Saturday ... I rang him up Saturday. "Come & see me on Sunday", was his answer. "I will see you & tell you my decision when I have made up my mind." Sunday evening I rang up. "The King has a conference & will speak to you later", was the answer. But he did not ring up.

'Monday morning [7th December] came. I rang up at 1.00. p.m. & my brother told me he might be able to see me that evening. I told him, "I must go to London but would come to the Fort when he wanted me." I did not go to London but waited. I sent a telephone message to the Fort to say that if I was wanted I would be at Royal Lodge. My brother rang me up at 10 minutes to 7.0 p.m. to say "Come & see me after dinner," I said, "No, I will come & see you at once." I was with him at 7.0 p.m. The awful & ghastly suspense of waiting was over'.

'I went back to Royal Lodge for dinner & returned to the Fort later. I felt having once got there I was not going to leave. As he is my eldest brother I had to be there to try & help him in his hour of need. I went back to London that night with my wife.'

The Duke and Duchess of York present new colours to the 4/5th Battalion of The Black Watch in August 1935 at Glamis Castle. With them are the two Princesses.

A barrier grew up between Mrs. Simpson and the Duchess, ever-protective for Bertie, until lifted at David's funeral.

The curious lack of communication between the King and the Duke of York has sometimes, but wrongly, been put down to an attempt to pass the crown to the Duke of Kent, who alone of his brothers then had a son. A moment's reflection would reveal how impossible this would have been, despite the weight attached to royal historian Dermot Morrah, who makes reference to it.

The throne is held by hereditary right and the Duke of York was heir presumptive according to the constitution. Nothing short of a series of unheard of renunciations could have changed this.

On Tuesday morning, 8th December when Bertie and Elizabeth knew that they were destined to reign, she became ill with influenza and was ordered to bed by her doctor. The Duke had to face the remainder of his ordeal alone. The next day, Wednesday, he drove back to Royal Lodge to meet Queen Mary and his brother, the King, as the Fort was besieged with reporters.

King Edward VIII's last act of kingship was to sign the Instrument of Abdication, which he did in the Drawing Room at the Fort at 10.00 a.m. Thursday 10th December. The Duke of York and his other brothers were witnesses. Edward's reign ended at 1.52 p.m. on the following day, Friday 11th December by the passing of the Declaration of Abdication Act. At 145 Piccadilly, the Duke and his family, by now rejoined by the Duchess, were having lunch, urgently waiting for a telephone call. Sir Maurice Hankey, Clerk of the Privy Council, rang up from the House of Lords to say, 'Will you tell His Majesty that he has just been proclaimed King.'

Bertie looked at his family, 'Now if someone comes through on the telephone, who shall I say I am.'

The new King's reign had begun and Elizabeth was his Queen.

A happy scene of twins curtseying to the Duchess after presenting their purse to her in aid of the National Council for Maternity and Child Welfare in July 1935 at a garden party at St. James's Palace.

Elizabeth The Queen

The Queen Consort has a special place in the British Constitution. She is the first Lady in the land, and bears the title of 'Her Majesty' for life. Elizabeth was also the last Empress of India. She has her own Household. This includes her Lord Chamberlain, Treasurer, Private Secretary, Mistress of the Robes and her ladies-in-waiting.

Queen Elizabeth chose for her Lord Chamberlain, the Earl of Airlie, son of Mabell, Countess of Airlie, for many years lady-in-waiting to Queen Mary. Lord Airlie's son, Angus Ogilvy later married the King and Queen's niece, Princess Alexandra of Kent.

The ladies-in-waiting are in two grades, the Ladies of the Bedchamber for the more formal duties, and the Women of the Bedchamber of whom at least one is always on duty in daily attendance on the Queen. The Duchess of Northumberland became her first Mistress of the Robes, the senior Lady who has special duties at a Coronation, and attends the Queen on state and other important occasions. One of the ladies-in-waiting of whom the Queen Mother was particularly fond, was Lady Helen Graham, who had been a lady-in-waiting since 1926 when the Queen was Duchess of York. She died in 1945.

The Queen's birthday was, and still is, celebrated by a salute of forty-one guns fired by the King's Troop, Royal Horse Artillery in Hyde Park and by a sixty-two gun salute fired by the Honourable Artillery Company in the Tower of London. All Government buildings hoist the Union Jack on her birthday. Since 1937 she has been eligible to perform the duties of a Counsellor of State in the absence or incapacity of the Sovereign, which has been continued in the present Queen's reign.

Queen Elizabeth has her own Standard of the Royal Arms impaled with those of the Bowes-Lyon family. When she was Queen Consort, the Standard was flown when she was present at Buckingham Palace without the King. The Queen Mother's Standard is now flown from any building where she is present. At the State Opening of Parliament the Queen's throne was placed level with that of the King.

The new King decided to reign as King George VI. Albert has a foreign ring about it, and was introduced to Britain by the Prince Consort. More importantly, he wished to base his reign on that of his father, King George V. Even their signatures were identical.

The British people accepted the new King with immediate relief. A return to his father's values was looked on just as if he had succeeded to the Throne on King George V's death. The only jarring note was Archbishop Lang's tactless broadcast after the former King's departure, which was considered to be 'kicking a man when he's down'.

Now Windsor Castle had recovered its position and Lady Diana Cooper recorded a dinner party there which finished at 10.30, when the guests went to bed.

The King said to his cousin, Lord Louis Mountbatten, on his first evening of reigning, 'Dickie, this is absolutely terrible. I never wanted this to happen, I'm quite unprepared for it. David has been trained for this all his life. I've never even seen a State Paper. I'm only a Naval Officer, it's the only thing I know about.' Lord Louis could reassure him. King George V, Bertie's father, had said much the same words to Dickie's father, Prince Louis of Battenberg, on the death of his brother the Duke of Clarence. Prince Louis then told him, 'George you're wrong. There is no more fitting preparation for a King than to have been trained in the Navy.'

One of the elements of a naval training is an ability to make snap decisions. One was required on the first afternoon. Sir John Reith

of the B.B.C. had to be told how to introduce the former King for his broadcast. Said the King, 'He cannot be Mr. Edward Windsor as he was born the son of a Duke'. On his specific instructions Reith announced 'His Royal Highness Prince Edward'.

Immediately the King and Queen found a new strength. She wrote to the Archbishop of Canterbury. 'I can hardly now believe that we have been called to this tremendous task and (I am writing to you quite intimately) the curious thing is that we are not afraid.'

After the King took his Oath at the Accession Council held at St. James's Palace on Saturday 12th December, he addressed his Privy Counsellors in a low clear voice but with many hesitations, 'With My wife and helpmate by My side, I take up the heavy task which lies before Me. In it I look for the support of all My peoples.'

Then, and only then, was he proclaimed King; despite what Sir Maurice Hankey had said the day before. With ancient ceremonial, Garter King of Arms, standing beside Bernard Fitzalan-Howard, Duke of Norfolk, hereditary Earl Marshal of England, proclaimed King George VI from the balcony overlooking Friary Court, St. James's Palace. This was

His Majesty King George VI in December 1936 after succeeding his brother King Edward VIII.

followed by three further ceremonies at Charing Cross, Temple Bar and from the steps of the Royal Exchange.

One of the King's first acts, three days after his accession, was to bestow on the Queen the Order of the Garter, the foremost Order of Chivalry. The Queen, highly delighted, wrote to Queen Mary, 'He had discovered that Papa gave it to you on his, Papa's birthday, June 3rd, and the coincidence was so charming that he has now followed suit, & given it to me on his own birthday.'

The transition from Duke of York to King also affected the little Princesses. Lady Cynthia Asquith, who had been invited to 145 Piccadilly, on 11th December, spoke of a letter on the hall table addressed to 'Her Majesty the Queen'. 'That's Mummy now, isn't it?' asked Princess Elizabeth. Other problems exercised her sister. Princess Margaret objected that she was no longer a Princess of York, 'and I have only just learnt to spell YORK'. She also asked her father, 'Do you sing, "God Save thy Gracious Me?"'

Madame Guèrin's daughter, Georgina, had come back to take charge of the Princesses during their first holiday after the Accession and became overawed by their parents' new

status. 'Everything is so different now. I feel quite shy with all of you.' The Queen smiled, 'only circumstances change, Georgina: people stay the same'.

Now that the ten-and-a-half-year-old Princess Elizabeth was heiress presumptive to the throne, she would need to be trained for that destiny so as not to suffer as her father had done. Sir John Wheeler-Bennett said that the King, remembering his own unhappy days of childhood, 'was determined that, come what might, Princess Elizabeth and Princess Margaret should look back upon their early years as a golden age'.

The Princesses already had diverse traits in character. Princess Elizabeth had some of the quiet reserve of her father, but showed signs of her parents' strong sense of duty. Princess Margaret had an extrovert personality, which has been described as being of 'sunshine and rain'. The King was particularly susceptible

to her charms. She sometimes jumped upon his knee, waiting to be cuddled, or would tickle him into fits of laughter. 'Margaret can charm the pearl out of an oyster', he proudly exclaimed.

Life changed overnight for the new King and Queen. After a 9.00 a.m. breakfast, he had to do a full day's work at his 'office', in Buckingham Palace, sometimes not finishing until 7.00 in the evening. Daily he had to go through his red despatch boxes of state papers. Then there were audiences of ministers, visiting ambassadors, and much paper work to catch up after the Abdication crisis. The King and Queen normally lunched and dined together, and only on rare occasions were they separated at night.

The formal move to Buckingham Palace took place on 17th February 1937. Mabell, Lady Airlie commented that the Queen's sitting room was already beginning to show

Handley Seymour of New Bond Street, and ten women of the Royal School of Needlework, one of her 'patronages', at their headquarters in Kensington, sat round a long table embroidering the Coronation Robe with emblems of the British Isles and Commonwealth. The dresses for the Queen's Maids of Honour were created by a new designer called Norman Hartnell.

To show solidarity, Queen Mary constantly appeared on numerous official occasions with the King and Queen. There was no precedent for a Queen Dowager to attend a Coronation after her own, but so eager was she to see her son crowned that she decided to waive this tradition. Both the King and Queen were delighted for her to attend.

At 3.00 on the morning of 12th May, Coronation Day, the King and Queen were awakened by the testing of loudspeakers on Constitution Hill. 'One of them might have been in our room', wrote the King. He had long been practising his breathing exercises, and was too nervous to eat any breakfast. The band of the Royal Marines woke Princess Elizabeth at 5.00 a.m., 'I leapt out of bed and so did Bobo', she said in her essay on the Coronation.

This was the first Coronation to be broadcast and filmed by cinema newsreels, but the new B.B.C. television cameras were not allowed to televise the Abbey Service.

At 10.00 that morning, amid intermittent showers, the great golden State Coach, built for George III in 1762 to open Parliament, and drawn by eight Windsor Greys, left Buckingham Palace to join a great cavalcade. Before and behind the coach were divisions of the Sovereign's Escort of the Household Cavalry, and on each side walked the Yeomen of the Guard. The King and Queen received a great ovation.

Both the Princesses travelled with Queen Mary, a regal figure dressed in purple and ermine, wearing glittering jewels and an open crown of diamonds. They received cheers that rivalled those for the King and Queen.

Queen Mary took her seat in the Royal Box in the Abbey between her sister-in-law, Queen Maud of Norway, and Princess Elizabeth, who sat next to her young sister. The Countess of Strathmore, proudly watching her daughter's Coronation, was next to Princess Marina, Duchess of Kent.

The whole of the first part of the 1000-year-old Coronation Service belonged to the King. The words of Dr. Lang, Archbishop of Canterbury, 'Sirs, I here present to you, King

Front view of Buckingham Palace facing the Mall, with the Queen Victoria Memorial and its famous red tulips in the foreground.

the traces of her own personality. 'It looks homelike already. The King, who had come in for a few minutes, smiled proudly ... "Elizabeth could make a home anywhere", he said.'

The quiet domestic life when they were Duke and Duchess of York immediately evaporated. No longer were they able to dine in public restaurants or dance at night clubs. Royal Lodge took on a new significance as a haven of privacy. As Windsor Castle was cold and uncomfortable, they normally relaxed at the Lodge as would any private family, sometimes entertaining their friends.

The King decided that Coronation Day planned for his brother on 12th May 1937 should remain unaltered. As there was less than five months to go instead of the usual period of three times that length, the Queen was immediately plunged into its preparation. Her Coronation dress was made by

Opposite:
State portrait of Her
Majesty Queen Elizabeth
wearing her Coronation
Robes, painted by Sir
Gerald Kelly.

George, your undoubted King', were answered with the chorus, 'God Save King George'. The actual solemn moment of his placing the Crown of St. Edward on the King's Head, was accompanied by the people shouting 'God Save the King'. The peers put on their coronets and the trumpets sounded.

Then came the Queen's Crowning. Supported by the Bishops of St. Albans and Blackburn, she made her way to the steps of the Altar and was anointed on the head with holy oil from the Ampulla, while four Duchesses, Norfolk, Rutland, Buccleuch and Roxburghe, held over her the Canopy of cloth of gold. The Archbishop of Canterbury placed on her fourth finger the Ring, and then on her head the Crown, containing the gleaming Koh-i-nor diamond, saying 'Receive the Crown of Glory, Honour and Joy'. At that solemn moment the peeresses all put on their coronets.

Princess Elizabeth and Princess Margaret both donned their little coronets of gold, which was the only time they wore them. Momentarily, the Queen looked up at the Royal Gallery, and only once did a faint smile cross her face. This was when Princess Margaret, leaning down from the Gallery, dropped a chocolate over the rail. The young Princess was very good. 'I had to nudge her once or twice', said the eleven-year-old Princess Elizabeth, 'when she played with "the Order of Service" too loudly.'

After the Coronation ended, the King and Queen went to a buffet luncheon in a canon's room and compared notes. The only mishap that had befallen the Queen was that a Presbyterian Minister had fainted in her procession, just as had happened at their wedding, but the King had long list of errors. The Dean tried to put on him the muslin under-garment, *Colobium Sindonis*, inside out; the Archbishop's thumb completely covered the printed words of the Oath he had to read; the Lord Great Chamberlain fumbled and could not fasten the belt of his Sword; and a red thread was missing which should have indicated the right way round of placing St. Edward's Crown on his head. 'I never did know whether it was right or not', he said afterwards. To cap it all, a Bishop stood on his Robe after leaving the Coronation Chair, nearly bringing him down. 'I had to tell him to get off it pretty sharply.'

In the afternoon the King and Queen, wearing their crowns, made their way in the great procession to Buckingham Palace, taking a longer route through the London streets. Though raining hard, this did not dampen the people's enthusiasm. Their Majesties appeared five times on the balcony at Buckingham Palace, the crowds remaining until after midnight. At eight that evening, the King spoke to the nation, 'The Queen and I will always keep in our hearts the inspiration of this day'. Such was the strain of the day, the Queen completely lost her voice.

In the days that followed the Coronation there were other processions, a State Banquet, a Ball, a review of 5,000 men and women of St. John Ambulance Brigade in Hyde Park, and a special dinner party given to the Indian Princes. This was the one and only time they met as a body with their last Emperor and Empress. Their Durbar, which was planned and postponed, never took place, and the Imperial title was relinquished in 1947. India, though now a Republic, elected to stay within the British Commonwealth.

On 20th May the King reviewed the Fleet at Spithead. This was the occasion when Lieutenant Commander Woodroffe, in a well-reported incident broadcast the famous description, 'the Fleet's all lit up'.

The Duke of Windsor married Mrs. Wallis Warfield, who had reverted to her maiden name, on 3rd June 1937 (George V's birthday) at the Château de Candé, near Tours. The former King had pointedly received royal status for himself only – he remained

Right:
A Coronation mug, the
most popular of the many
souvenirs to celebrate the
Coronation.

Illustrated cover of a souvenir booklet published to commemorate the Coronation, price one shilling.

For the State Visit of King Leopold of the Belgians that November, Norman Hartnell was invited to design the Queen's dress. The King took him round the galleries, observing on the beauty of pictures by Winterhalter. He took the hint and designed 'a *robe de style* of gleaming silver tissue over a hooped *carcase* of stiffened silver gauze, with a deep *berthe* collar of silver lace encrusted with glittering diamonds'. This was such an outstanding success that Hartnell was launched as the Royal couturier.

The year ended with the traditional Sandringham Christmas. The King and Queen established themselves in their first twelve months' reign. Both showed an air of confidence not seen before. Much of their success was due to the personality of the Queen but it would be a mistake to suppose that the King always leaned on her. Her sister Lady Elphinstone said, 'they were so particularly together; they both leant so much on the other'. But in the words of her other sister Lady Granville, 'in fundamental things she leant on him: I have always felt how much the Queen was sustained by the King'.

A State Visit to France was planned to begin on 28th June 1938, but on the 22nd, her brother David telephoned to break the news that their mother had had a severe heart attack. She had been unwell for some time and the Queen used to visit her at their flat in Cumberland Mansions, Portman Square, at least twice a week. Lady Strathmore died at 2.00 the following morning. She was charming, wise and possessed great courage. The Queen Mother has based her character on her mother's, and her death was a great blow to her.

President Lebrun at once suggested that the State Visit should be postponed for three weeks. It was Norman Hartnell who explained to the Queen that white was a suitable colour for mourning, and at the same time would be chic. Within fourteen days her entire collection of thirty afternoon dresses and evening gowns were altered into white.

Though the King and Queen had visited Paris for three official visits when Duke and Duchess of York, this was the first State Visit there since 1914, when King George V and Queen Mary came. This proved an overwhelming success both in its grandeur and on the importance of the occasion: the meeting of the heads of state of two great allies in a Europe on the brink of war. Who could then have foretold of the collapse of France less than two years later.

bitter all his life that his wife could not share that status. Ironically this was announced on the same day that the Prime Minister during the abdication crisis, Stanley Baldwin, was rewarded with the title of Earl Baldwin of Bewdley. His successor as Prime Minister was Neville Chamberlain.

In July the King and Queen visited Edinburgh. As this was the first time for centuries that a Scottish Queen had entered the city, the people went wild with joy. An eighty-four-year-old Highlander made her smile when he told her, 'You're a bonnie lassie. I wish I'd courted you myself'.

The King bestowed on the Queen the Order of the Thistle in St. Giles's Cathedral. He had given her as his Coronation present, a superb Thistle Badge and Star, of fine South African diamonds. He joked, 'We have only one Thistle. I wear it one night, the Queen the next.'

The Parisians gave the King and Queen a great welcome, entertaining their guests with banquets, receptions and balls. Lady Diana Cooper wrote, 'Each night's flourish outdid the last'. The visit ended with a brilliant reception at the Quai d'Orsay. Violet Trefusis, a guest, described how, in spite of the tight security, the King and Queen, without consulting anyone, came out on to the balcony, hand in hand. The people in Paris went mad with delight.

On their way home the Royal couple went to Villers-Bretonneux, near Amiens, to unveil a memorial to the 11,000 Australians who fell in the war without a known grave. The Queen walked forward and laid an armful of poppies. They had been picked that morning by a boy who gave them to her. Madame Lebrun wrote to the Queen, 'I wish to assure your Majesty that she has won the heart of the whole of Paris'.

The year 1938 was one of a succession of crises. Austria was seized by Hitler in February, and Czechoslovakia was under threat. Trenches were being dug in London parks and gas masks began to be issued. In September the gravity of the situation kept the King in London and on the 27th the mobilization of the Fleet was ordered. He was to have accompanied the Queen on 27th September to Clydeside to launch Cunard's largest ship in the world, the 82,998-ton R.M.S. *Queen Elizabeth*, but the Queen had to travel alone in his stead. The Princesses joined her in Glasgow.

At the launching from John Brown's Shipyard that afternoon, the Queen said in a clear voice, 'I have a message to you from the King. He bids the people of this country to be of good cheer, in spite of the dark clouds hanging over them, and indeed over the whole world. He knows well that, as ever before in critical times, they will keep cool heads and brave hearts; he knows too, that they will place entire confidence in their leaders who, under God's providence, are striving their utmost to find a just and peaceful solution to the grave problems which confront them.'

The day after the launching, 28th September, was 'Black Wednesday', expected by many people to have been the last day of peace. On the next day Neville Chamberlain flew off to Munich to meet Hitler for the second time. He came back in triumph to Heston Airport on the 30th, waving the text of his agreement, 'peace in our time'. But within weeks, this feeling of security had passed.

When the Queen was reunited with her husband he showed her a cordial invitation from President Roosevelt, for them to visit the United States, adding 'If you bring either or both of the children with you they will also

Coronation Luncheon for King George VI and Queen Elizabeth at the Guildhall, painted by Frank Salisbury.

be very welcome, and I shall try and have one or two Roosevelts of approximately the same age to play with them!'

Mr. Mackenzie King, the Canadian Prime Minister, had already invited the King and Queen to visit Canada when he was in Britain for the Coronation. At first the King was doubtful that he should be away at a time of great emergency, but felt the importance of strengthening ties with Canada and the United States justified his going. Instead of sailing in the battle cruiser H.M.S. *Repulse*, as planned, he substituted the Canadian Pacific liner, *Empress of Australia*, which would sail under the White Ensign. He and the Queen reluctantly left the Princesses behind.

The King and Queen sailed from Portsmouth on the afternoon of 6th May. Queen Mary brought the Princesses to see them sail. The Queen's last words to Princess Elizabeth aboard the liner, as the two children were going ashore, were 'Be good and look after Margaret'. After a delayed but not uneventful voyage, the Queen wrote to her mother-in-law, Queen Mary, 'For three & a half days we only moved a few miles. The fog was so thick, that it was like a white cloud round the ship and the foghorn blew incessantly. Its melancholy blasts were echoed back by the icebergs like the twang of a piece of wire. Incredibly eery [sic], and really very alarming, knowing that we were surrounded by ice & unable to see a foot either way.

'We very nearly hit a berg the day before yesterday, and the poor Captain was nearly demented because some kind cheerful people kept on reminding him that it was about here that the *Titanic* was struck, & *just* about the same date!' She was heard to say, 'it is almost like being Arctic explorers'. While the King commented 'I should not have chosen an ice field surrounded by dense fog in which to have a holiday, but it does seem to be the only place for me to rest in nowadays!!'

They landed at Wolfe's Bay, Quebec, at 10.30 a.m. on 17th May, two days' late. Every day was filled with engagements, but the magnitude of their success was phenomenal. 'A Queen who smiled like an angel' was a typical newspaper banner headline.

The King opened the Canadian Parliament at Ottawa and in their six weeks' tour from coast to coast they covered 7242 kilometres (4,500 miles). Lord Tweedsmuir, the Governor-General, better known as John Buchan the author, wrote to a friend in Scotland, of the impact they made: 'The visit is going to have an enormous effect in Canada and in the

United States, and, indeed, on the whole world, as a demonstration of our unity of spirit ... As for the Queen, she has a perfect genius for the right kind of publicity....

'At the unveiling of the War Memorial, where we had some 10,000 veterans, she asked me if it was not possible to get a little closer to them. I suggested that we went right down among them, if they were prepared to take the risk, which they gladly did. It was an amazing sight, for we were simply swallowed up ... The American correspondents were simply staggered. They said that no American President would ever have dared to do that. It was a wonderful example of what true democracy means, and a people's King.'

They visited Victoria, capital of British Columbia, 'more British than the British'. Here a guard of honour was formed of forty-five men from the county of Angus, including six who had worked on the Glamis estate for her father, Lord Strathmore. They spent a night in a log cabin, Outlook Cabin, in Jasper Park Lodge. To settle an argument, the Queen was asked whether she was Scottish or English. 'Since we reached Quebec', she replied, 'I've been a Canadian.'

As always, the King was interested in uniforms and regalia. Noticing a Mayor without his chain of office, he asked the Mayor's wife whether he possessed one. If not, he would like to present him with a chain. 'Yes, he has', she replied, 'but he only wears it on *important* occasions.' This became a Royal family joke. When dressed up in particular finery, they used to ask each other, 'Is it an *important* occasion?'

At the end of the Canadian tour came the three-day visit to the United States. King George VI was the first British Sovereign to set foot on American soil. They crossed the border on the night of 7th June, and at 11.00 on the following morning they were met by Mr. and Mrs. F.D. Roosevelt at Washington Station, in the midst of a heatwave of 36°C (97°F). Mrs. Roosevelt noted in her diary, 'in the course of a long life I have seen many important events in Washington, but never have I seen crowds such as lined the whole route between the Union Station and the White House.'

The Roosevelts became firm friends of the King and Queen during the visit, which helped in bringing the two nations together.

One little girl, the eight-year-old daughter of Harry Hopkins, the President's Special Adviser and a friend of F.D.R's grandchildren, expressed her disbelief in the Royal guests. 'They are not like the King and Queen of my fairy tales', she complained. On hearing this, the Queen asked if the child might sit up late to see them depart for a banquet at the Embassy. Seeing the Queen in her beautiful crinoline, jewels and diadem, the little girl curtsied to her and said, 'Oh, Daddy, Daddy, I have seen the Fairy Queen!' She quite ignored the King!

The ladies of Washington came in all their finery to a garden party at the British Embassy. The Queen appeared cool under a dainty parasol of white, lined with green *crêpe*. Parasols immediately became the height of fashion.

From the White House the President took his guests for a trip down the Potomac River to see Mount Vernon, George Washington's home. This was of special interest to the Queen, who said it was one of the loveliest places that she had ever seen. Sir Anthony Wagner, now Clarenceux King of Arms at the College of Arms, but then a young Pursuivant, had just made an interesting discovery.

The Queen Mother not only descends from several early pioneers of Virginia, but is one of the nearest living relations of George Washington, the first American President. Mary Warner, a daughter of Colonel Augustine Warner of Warner Hall, Gloucester County, Virginia, was an ancestress of the 13th Earl of Strathmore and thus of Queen Elizabeth. Her sister, Mildred Warner, married Lawrence Washington, and was George Washington's grandmother.

From the City of Washington the King and Queen visited New York where they

President and Mrs. Franklin D. Roosevelt wave goodbye to the King and Queen from their Hyde Park home, New York on their leaving for Canada in June 1939.

received a fantastic ticker-tape welcome, and then went to the World Fair. She commented on their rousing welcome to Mayor Fiorello La Guardia, 'there is nothing nicer in the world than friendship'. Once again 'Queen Liz' hit the headlines. Columnists nominated her 'the Woman of the Year'.

On the evening of 10th June the Roosevelts had gone ahead to Hyde Park, their ancestral home since 1819, situated on the steep bank of the Hudson River, 145 kilometres (90 miles) from New York. Here, with his aged mother, Mrs. Sara Delano Roosevelt, they waited to receive their Royal guests for the night.

Due at 6.00 p.m., it was nearly 8.00 before they arrived, being delayed at the Fair. The President smiled as he told the King, 'Mother doesn't approve of cocktails. She thinks that as you come from England you'd prefer a cup of tea.' He and the King then took a large glass. The King told him, 'My mother doesn't approve of cocktails either.'

There must have been a jinx on their stay at Hyde Park. The President brought his coloured staff to help from the White House. The English butler, incensed, walked out. In the middle of the meal a side-table collapsed and part of the dinner service crashed to the ground. Silence was broken when one of the President's daughters-in-law exclaimed, 'I hope none of *my* dishes were broken', followed by laughter.

After dinner, when the party had gone to the library, there was a second great crash. The coloured butler missed a step into the room. Decanters, bottles, glasses and ice-cubes all fell headlong, leaving a large pool in the middle of the floor. The King and Queen were secretly amused, as they always were when plans suddenly go awry.

The party did not break up until 1.30 in the morning. F.D.R. placed his hand on the King's knee, saying 'Young man, it's time for you to go to bed'. But he did not go straight to bed. Upstairs Mackenzie King, who was also a guest, and he thrashed out some vital issues.

On the evening of 11th June the King and Queen returned to Canada. Mrs. Roosevelt wrote: 'As the train pulled out, somebody began singing "Auld Lang Syne" and then everyone was singing, and it seemed to me that there was something of our friendship and our sadness and something of the uncertainty of our futures in that song that could not have been said in any other words. I think the King and Queen, standing on the rear

platform of the train as it pulled slowly away, were deeply moved. I know I was.'

At 8.20 a.m. on 15th June they sailed, this time in the *Empress of Britain*, from Halifax, Nova Scotia amidst wildly cheering crowds. According to her lady-in-waiting, 'The Queen was really exhausted by the time we left for home, but she would never say she found anything tiring, and she always brushed off any reference to her fatigue.'

The Princesses were taken on board the destroyer, *Kempenfelt* on 22nd June to meet their parents on board *Empress of Britain*. This had been their second long parting from Princess Elizabeth, although she would not have remembered the 1927 tour. When they all returned to Waterloo that evening they received a welcome rivalling the Coronation. Excitedly Sir Harold Nicolson told his wife, Vita, of the stirring reception in Parliament Square, as they passed by. 'There were the King and Queen and the two princesses. We lost all our dignity and yelled and yelled. The King wore a happy schoolboy grin. The Queen was superb. She really does manage to convey to each individual in the crowd that he or she have had a personal greeting. It is due, I think, to the brilliance of her eyes. But she is in truth one of the most amazing Queens since Cleopatra. We returned to the House with lumps in our throats.'

In July the King and Queen went to the Royal Naval College, Dartmouth to see their preparations for the emergency. They travelled in the Royal Yacht, *Victoria and Albert*, with Lord Louis Mountbatten as A.D.C. His nephew, Prince Philip of Greece, was deputed as Captain's Messenger of the day to look after the Princesses. Despite Crawfie's (Marion Crawford) words that 'Princess Elizabeth never took her eyes off him the whole time', apparently the visit did not have any particular significance either to the thirteen-year-old Princess or the eighteen-year-old cadet.

While the King and Queen were over in America and indeed until that August there was a false feeling of security. He held the last of his Duke of York Camps at Abergeldie, taking the boys over to Balmoral for tea and then he took the Princesses to the camp for supper. On 23rd August the world gasped at yet one more crisis, the Soviet-German non-aggression pact, which made the King hurry back to London. Five days later the Queen left her daughters in the care of her Treasurer, Sir Basil Brooke. 'I must be with the King', she said. The King arranged for the

Princesses to be taken to Birkhall. Nine-year-old Princess Margaret got impatient with all these changes of plan. 'Who is this Hitler spoiling everything?' Their parents used to telephone them every evening at 6.00.

War was now a week away. The Queen heard from Queen Mary, 'I feel deeply for you. I having gone through all this in August 1914 when I was the wife of the Sovereign.'

The ultimatum to Germany expired at 11.00 a.m. Sunday 3rd September 1939. The Queen was immediately immersed in war work. She became Commander-in-Chief of the Women's Royal Naval Service (W.R.N.S.), the Auxiliary Territorial Service (A.T.S.) and the Women's Auxiliary Air Force (W.A.A.F.), but it was particularly at the King's wish that she did not wear their uniform. One of her main concerns was in the facilities for evacuated mothers and children.

The King and Queen were reunited with their daughters for Christmas at Sandringham, the last time they used 'the big house'. Afterwards they went to Appleton House or a smaller house on the estate. The Princesses stayed until February. They then went to Royal Lodge, but were removed for greater

Above:
The Queen and the Princesses going down the steps at Windsor Castle in 1941.

Overleaf:
An aerial view of Balmoral Castle under snow.

safety to Windsor Castle in May when the enemy amassed across the Channel. Officially they were 'somewhere in the country'. Here they remained throughout the war, having the great advantage of not being cut off by distance from their parents.

When friends suggested to the Queen that she should send the Princesses to safety in America, she replied, 'The children could not go without me. I won't leave the King, and of course the King will never leave'. She told Sir Harold Nicolson, 'I should die if I had to leave'. Instead she began to train with a revolver. Sir Harold told his wife, 'I cannot tell you how superb she was. . . . What astonished me is how the King is changed. He is now like his brother. He was so gay and she so calm. They did me all the good in the world . . . We *shall win*; I know that, I have no doubts at all.'

In the King's first Christmas Day broadcast of the war he immortalized a moving poem 'The Gate of the Year' by Marie Louise Haskins, a retired lecturer of the London School of Economics, which had been sent to him:

> 'I said to the man who stood at the Gate of the Year,
>> "Give me a light that I may tread safely into the unknown."
> 'And he replied:
>> "Go out into the darkness, and put your hand into the hand of God. That shall be to you better than a light, and safer than a known way."'

The poem appears on bronze plaques on the entry gates to the King George VI Memorial Chapel, at the side of St. George's Chapel, Windsor.

On 9th April 1940 the Germans invaded Denmark and Norway, quickly followed on 10th May by Holland and Belgium. These small countries were quickly over-run, and on 13th May, Princess Juliana of the Netherlands was brought by her husband Prince Bernhard, who at once returned to fight with the resistance. Juliana's mother, Queen

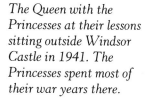

The Queen with the Princesses at their lessons sitting outside Windsor Castle in 1941. The Princesses spent most of their war years there.

Wilhelmina, arrived at Harwich on the same day with only the clothes she had on, escaping in a British destroyer. The Queen later stood as godmother to Irene, Princess Juliana's daughter, who was christened in the Chapel at Buckingham Palace, the last before it was destroyed by a bomb. The Dutch Royal Family then sought sanctuary in Canada. Three weeks later King Haakon and Crown Prince Olav of Norway arrived, leaving only King Christian of Denmark and King Leopold of the Belgians remaining with their people. Buckingham Palace became the haven of exiled monarchs. Leopold's decision resulted in much uninformed criticism against his conduct in the war, in which the King and Queen did not join. She must have been pleased at his complete vindication before his death in 1983.

In May 1940 Winston Churchill became Prime Minister, and in June, France fell. On the 14th the Queen gave one of her most impressive broadcasts, to the women of France. Speaking in French, as one who has 'always loved France so warmly', she said, 'I share your suffering today and feel it.' She concluded, 'A nation defended by such men and loved by such women must sooner or later attain victory.'

The London blitz began in September. On Friday the 13th a stick of six bombs was dropped right across the Palace. Two exploded in the quadrangle, making a resounding crash about 27m (30yd) from the King and Queen. A third bomb fell just beyond them at the side of the wing in which they had both been standing, destroying the Chapel. The King and Queen had been talking to his Private Secretary, Alec Hardinge, a brother of the Queen's great friend the late Diamond Hardinge. They had been in his little sitting room. 'We were out into the passage as fast as we could get there', wrote the King. 'The whole thing happened in a matter of seconds. We all wondered why we weren't dead.' Had the windows been closed, all the glass would have splintered into their faces, inflicting terrible injuries.

The Queen receiving two grey horses, a gift from Queen Wilhelmina of the Netherlands in 1946 at Buckingham Palace.

They went down to the basement and checked that the staff sheltering there were safe. The Queen joked with a policeman on the scene, and added, 'I'm glad we've been bombed. Now I can look the East End in the face'. Today the Queen Mother suspects that the unexploded bomb, which probably fell in the garden, may still be there.

Their old house, 145 Piccadilly, received a direct hit in one of the early raids.

The King and Queen travelled to the worst blitzed areas throughout the country. As Winston Churchill said, 'Many an aching heart found some solace in her gracious smile'. Her duties often extended to sixteen or seventeen hours a day, and she seldom reached her bed before midnight. She ran sewing parties twice a week in the Blue Drawing Room at Buckingham Palace. The Cabinet recommended that they should get back to Windsor each night for safety's sake.

The Queen had another lucky escape at Windsor, this time from an encounter with a deserter. While dressing for dinner, a man sprang at her in her bedroom from behind a curtain. He flung himself on her, seizing her around the ankles. 'For a moment my heart stood absolutely still', she said, but soon realized that the man was demented and would attack her if she screamed. She said

quietly 'tell me about it'. The man poured out his story to her as she rose quietly and rang a bell. His family had all been killed in an air-raid and he had deserted. 'Poor man, I felt so sorry for him', she said. 'I realized quickly that he did not mean any harm.' The man proved to be a temporary employee of a firm doing some work at the Castle.

The Queen had a remarkable cousin, Lilian Bowes-Lyon who, early in the blitz on London, moved into a tiny flat in Bow Road, Poplar, one of the worst-hit areas in the East End. Here she worked day and night to nurse the wounded and help the homeless, frequently having to pull bodies out of the rubble. 'Florence Nightingale of the East End', the Bow people called her. The Queen and the Duke of Kent both came to see her in that little flat and helped behind the scenes. Throughout all this heroic work, she was suffering from diabetes and was crippled with arthritis. She lost a leg and eventually her life as the result of a bombing accident.

Both the King and Queen suffered bereavements in the war. The Queen's nephew, John Patrick Bowes-Lyon, Master of Glamis, was killed in action in 1941 at Halfaya Pass. In August 1942, while dining at Balmoral, the King was called to the telephone and told that his youngest brother George, Duke of

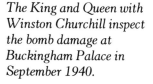

The King and Queen with Winston Churchill inspect the bomb damage at Buckingham Palace in September 1940.

The King and Queen at home in Buckingham Palace during 1942.

Kent, had been killed in an air crash in Scotland on his way to Iceland on duty with the R.A.F. This proved a great shock, as he and the Queen were devoted to him.

Queen Mary was given the sad news at Badminton, where she spent all her war years with her niece the Duchess of Beaufort and the Duke. When told, she said 'I must go to Marina at once'. The Duke of Kent was believed to have been arranging a meeting with a United States Air Force General in Iceland for future liaison duties. He was a great friend of President Roosevelt, who was godfather to his second son born seven weeks earlier and had the President's name added to his others, Michael George Charles Franklin.

Mrs. Eleanor Roosevelt had long wished to come over to England to see at first hand how the people were standing up to the war – into which the United States had entered in December 1941 when Pearl Harbor was bombed. She noted, 'there is a very remote chance that sometime F.D.R. may let me go to England this summer [1942] or autumn or winter if by doing so I can serve some good purpose both there and here.'

She was invited to Buckingham Palace, and when she arrived she was shown up to the Queen's own bedroom on the first floor. 'An enormous room', she noted, 'without any windows having glass'. She wrote that 'Buckingham Palace is an enormous place, and without heat. I do not see how they keep the dampness out. The rooms were cold except for the smaller sitting-room with an open fire.'

That evening they dined on gold and silver plates, but 'nothing was ever served that was not served in any war canteen'. On the next day they drove through the East End of London when the Queen remarked, 'the only solace in the destruction was that new housing would replace the slums.'

Mrs. Roosevelt spent a weekend at Windsor Castle. 'After Queen Mary had gone to bed, the house party played "the Game", [a form of charades]', 'Chips' Channon commented, 'and became quite childish, with the Queen wearing a beard!'

Mrs. Roosevelt returned to America with the realization that England's home front formed part of the battle front. The King and Queen were not destined to meet F.D.R. in England. He and his wife had been warmly invited to come over just before his sudden death in April 1945.

At Windsor 'we now sit and eat in the Equerries' room at night', wrote a lady-in-

Above:
The Queen visits the London Headquarters of the Canadian Red Cross in July 1942 and chats to Canadian soldiers who form the guard of honour.

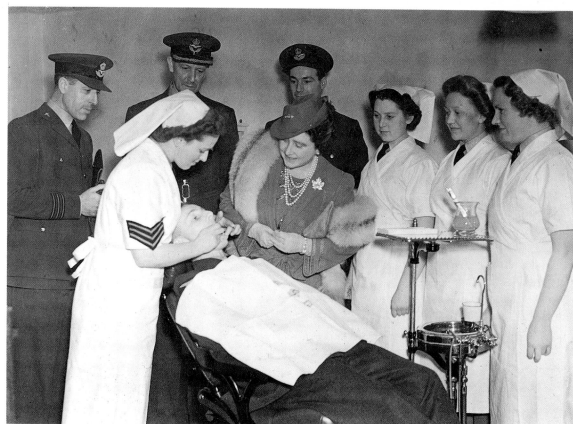

On a visit to the Air Crew Receiving Centre in London, the Queen watches the work of the Dental Section.

waiting, 'and the King and Queen eat in the Star Chamber next door. They always come in for a gossip before going to bed.' A small but strong cellar was reinforced and divided into two. The King and Queen slept in one compartment, and the Princesses and Alla in the other.

There were lighter interludes. The Princesses' Windsor pantomines were elaborate affairs, such as *Cinderella*, with Princess Elizabeth as Prince Charming and Princess Margaret as Cinderella. The King made sure that Princess Elizabeth's tunic was exactly right. Prince Philip was a guest for the 1943 production of *Aladdin*, where Princess Elizabeth made her entrance popping out of a laundry basket. The last pantomine *Old Mother Red Riding Boots* in 1944 was a mixture of half-a-dozen traditional stories, in which they sang the unforgettable 'sur le pont d'Avignon' as a traditional song, and then in swing time. Vera Lynn and Tommy Trinder were regular entertainers at the Castle.

The King and Queen, like their subjects, had their favourite radio programme, such as ITMA (It's that Man Again) and Much-Binding-in-the-Marsh. He told Tommy Handley of ITMA that the records made when he appeared at a Command Performance at Windsor Castle were played so often that they wore out. Once the Ministry of Information wanted to distribute Royal photographs of ITMA, but nothing would go right. Finally, the Queen suggested a picture of the King sitting at his desk telephoning. He picked up the receiver and said in a deep voice 'this is *Funf* speaking' (the ITMA catchphrase). Everyone burst into laughter and the photographers got their pictures.

In London, whenever the Queen had the opportunity, she used to attend the National Gallery Lunch Hour Concerts and listen to Dame Myra Hess and other pianists.

The King made a secret flight to see his victorious troops in North Africa in June 1943. The worried Queen confided in Queen Mary, 'I have had an anxious few hours, because at 8.15 I heard that the plane had been heard near Gibraltar, and that it would soon be landing. Then after an hour & a half I heard that there was a thick fog at Gib, & that they were going on to Africa. Then complete silence till a few minutes ago, when a message came that they had landed in Africa, & taken off again. Of course I imagined every sort of horror, & walked up & down my room staring at the telephone.'

Before the King left, the Queen had been appointed a Counsellor of State and, as such, held an investiture at Buckingham Palace. This included 300 men and women who received decorations for bravery in the war. The ceremony took much longer than usual, said the Lord Chamberlain, due to her talking at length to all the recipients. Punctuality gave way to expediency!

Prince Philip stayed at Balmoral in 1944, when Princess Elizabeth was eighteen. Philip's cousin, King George of Greece, had written to the King to express the hope that he would consider the young man as a prospective son-in-law. The King wrote back to say that he liked the Prince but Elizabeth was still too young. He also told Queen Mary, adding that 'she has never met any young men of her own age'. Queen Mary told Lady Airlie, 'I suppose my son is wise. After all he

As Patron of the Heritage Craft School at Chailey in Sussex, the Queen takes the Princesses to visit them in 1945.

had to wait long enough for *his* wife, and you can see what a success their marriage is.'

During the autumn 1944, Lord Strathmore's health began to cause anxiety. He was aged eighty-nine when he died at Glamis Castle on 7th November 1944, which was another sad loss to the Queen. A friend of the family writing in *The Times*, called him 'an embodiment of the noblest qualities of British aristocracy'. At his funeral at Glamis the pipers of The Black Watch played the poignant 'Flowers of the Forest'.

As a relief to the Queen's engagements connected with the war, there was one that particularly appealed to her. In 1944 the Treasurer of the Middle Temple approached her to become a Bencher, an appointment without precedent for a King or Queen. The Queen was pleased to accept, and was also the first woman to be admitted. She dined with her fellow Benchers in December 1944.

Five years later she became Treasurer of the Middle Temple.

On Sunday 6th May 1945 when the King and Queen were at Windsor, a message came that the unconditional German surrender was expected. They drove straight to London. Mr. Churchill made the official statement on 8th May, V.E. Day. A quarter of a million people surrounded the Palace, chanting 'We want the King. We want the Queen!' They appeared on the balcony eight times that evening, sometimes with Winston Churchill, sometimes with the Princesses, the last just before midnight.

The Princesses had been given permission to leave by a side door to join the sea of people below with their uncle David Bowes-Lyon and others, but the King drew the line at their going to Piccadilly Circus. When they returned the Queen provided them with sandwiches she had cut herself.

The King opened his first peacetime parliament for seven years on 13th August amid the jubilation of V.J. Day, for news of Japan's unconditional surrender had only just been received. Indeed, for the first time in history two Speeches from the Throne were prepared, one for use if the surrender was unconfirmed. That afternoon and evening the King and Queen appeared on the balcony a half-a-dozen times in response to the cheering multitudes.

The King broadcast to his people that evening. 'The war is over. You know, I think, that those four words have, for the Queen and myself, the same significance, simple yet immense, that they have for you. Our hearts are full to overflowing, as are your own. Yet there is not one of us who has experienced this terrible war who does not realize that we shall feel its inevitable consequence long after we have all forgotten our rejoicings of today.'

In January 1946 the King wrote from Sandringham to his brother the Duke of Gloucester, then Governor-General of Australia: 'I have been suffering from an awful reaction from the strain of the war I suppose & have felt very tired especially down here ... I am perfectly well really but feel that I cannot cope competently with all the varied & many questions which come up.'

Ten months after V.J. Day, came the Victory Parade of 9th June 1946, the largest military parade ever to be held in Britain. All the Allies participated, except Russia, Poland and Yugoslavia, who declined. In all there were 21,000 troops and civilians. The King took the salute from the dais and at his side was the Queen. Others in the Royal party were Queen Mary, Princess Elizabeth, in her A.T.S. uniform, and Princess Margaret. On the benches beside the dais were the Prime Minister, Clement Attlee, who had won the

The Queen talks to Allied soldiers and airmen at a Buckingham Palace garden party given in 1945 for repatriated prisoners of war.

Opposite:
Walking through the
garden of Royal Lodge,
the King and Queen with
the Princesses. Princess
Elizabeth bends to pat
'Chin', her Tibetan lion
dog, July 1946.

Below:
The King takes the salute
at the Victory Parade on
8th June 1946, with the
Queen, Queen Mary and
the Princesses on the
Royal dais. The Prime
Minister, Clement Attlee
and Winston Churchill
stand nearby.

July 1945 election, and Winston Churchill, architect of victory.

In August 1946 Princess Elizabeth became unofficially engaged to her cousin Prince Philip, but the King and Queen decided not to announce the news until their return from a tour of South Africa in the next spring. When Field Marshal Jan Smuts first invited them, the King was uncertain, being aware of the ill-feeling of many of the Dutch South Africans towards Britain. However, the King and Queen, with the Princesses, sailed in H.M.S. *Vanguard* bound for Cape Town on 1st February 1947. For the first time all four members of the immediate Royal Family, embarked together on their two weeks' tour.

When sixteen degrees of frost was reported in London, the coldest for a century, only Mr. Attlee could dissuade the King from flying home to be with his people in the middle of a coal crisis.

There were times on the tour when the King looked very tired. He first suffered from cramp in his legs and lost nearly a stone in weight. This he put down to the arduous nature of the tour. The heat sometimes

worried him, almost beyond endurance. At times he had 'gnashes' at the Household and others. A spectator noticed the Queen stroking his arm to calm him during an incredibly slow parade. Lady Longford tells a delightful story, that the King was justifiably infuriated by the Nationalists' hostility to Smuts. He burst out to the Queen 'I'd like to shoot them all!' To which she replied soothingly, 'but Bertie, you can't shoot them *all.*'

The South African trip, which extended to Rhodesia (now Zimbabwe), proved a great success, and was witnessed by all communities and colours. The Royal party travelled 16,000 kilometres (10,000 miles) up country in their special White Train. 'I remember standing in the corridor watching the Queen in a beautiful crinoline dress, sliding along the narrow corridor', said a lady-in-waiting, 'and how superbly she stepped down on to the platform and out among the waiting people. The Queen once remarked to me "You must *never* look at your feet. My mother always taught me that".'

One disgruntled old Afrikaner told the Queen, 'Pleased to have met you, Ma'am, but

we still feel sometimes that we can't forgive the English for conquering us.' 'I understand perfectly,' replied the Queen, with her disarming smile, 'We feel very much the same in Scotland.'

Princess Elizabeth celebrated her twenty-first birthday at Cape Town with a ball at Government House, dancing into the small hours of the morning. Earlier that evening she made a moving broadcast to the Commonwealth in which she dedicated her life to its service. The Royal party returned to England in May, to the Princess's special excitement. On 8th June she said to a friend, 'Something is going to happen at last. He is coming to-night!' The Royal engagement was announced at midnight.

On the following day the King and Queen gave a Garden Party at Buckingham Palace, and it was Philip Mountbatten's first public appearance with the Royal Family. That evening the crowds flocked into the Mall, singing 'All the Nice Girls love a Sailor'.

Prince Philip had become a naturalized citizen of the United Kingdom in February (the wheels were only set in motion again after the war ended), when he had to abandon his foreign titles and adopt a surname. He took the advice of Mr. Chuter Ede, the Home Secretary, becoming Lieutenant Philip Mountbatten, R.N., his mother's maiden name, translated from Battenberg.

On the wedding eve, the King gave Philip, the title, style and attribute of 'H.R.H.' and

At Royal Lodge, Windsor, the Queen with Princess Elizabeth who is mounted on a horse, July 1946.

on the day itself, the Dukedom of Edinburgh. Purists objected to his being called 'Prince Philip' as he was known at court, because the word 'Prince' had been omitted from the creation. But to his dying day the King believed that he had made his son-in-law a Prince. The Queen formally corrected this in 1957, but I make no apology for calling him a Prince from the time of his wedding, for the title of H.R.H. is meaningless unless it means the status of being a prince.

The wedding was celebrated at Westminster Abbey on 20th November 1947, amid rejoicing, but at a time of austerity and rationing. 'A flash of colour', said Winston Churchill, 'on the hard road we have to travel.' However there was one of the largest gatherings of royal guests assembled in modern times. 'A week of gaiety such as the Court has not seen for years', wrote Lady Airlie.

The King wrote to Princess Elizabeth on her honeymoon, 'I was so proud of you & thrilled at having you so close to me on our long walk in Westminster Abbey, but when I handed your hand to the Archbishop I felt that I had lost something very precious . . . I am so glad you wrote & told Mummy that you think the long wait before your engagement & the long time before the wedding was for the best. I was rather afraid that you had thought I was being hard hearted about it. . . .

'I have watched you grow up all these years with pride under the skilful direction of Mummy, who as you know is the most marvellous person in the world in my eyes, &

During the 1947 Royal tour of South Africa the King and Queen and Princesses visit Natal's National Park. They are seen here with General Smuts.

I can, I know, always count on you, & now Philip, to help us in our work.' The King once said 'We are not a family; we are a firm', and now the firm had a new junior partner.

On St. George's Day, 23rd April 1948, the 600th anniversary of the foundation of the Order of the Garter, the King installed Princess Elizabeth and her husband Prince Philip, as a Lady and Knight of the Garter. For the first time they took their places, resplendent in their robes, including the blue velvet mantle emblazoned with the red cross of St. George, and black hat with ostrich feathers, in the procession down to St. George's Chapel, Windsor with the King, Sovereign of the Order, and the Queen.

Three days later, the King and Queen celebrated their Silver Wedding, which again proved an occasion of a great and spontaneous demonstration of affection. For once in broad sunshine, with Princess Margaret, they left Buckingham Palace at 11.00 a.m. in a State Landau drawn by six Windsor Greys, for a Service of Thanksgiving in St. Paul's Cathedral. Princess Elizabeth and Prince Philip followed in another landau.

In the evening, after a long drive through London streets, and inevitably ending on the balcony of Buckingham Palace, they both broadcast to the nation.

The Queen said, 'I, too, am deeply thankful for our twenty-five years of happiness together, for the opportunities we have been given of service to our beloved country and for the blessings of our home and children. The world of our day is longing to find the secret of community, and all married lives are, in a sense, communities in miniature . . . Looking back over the last twenty-five years and to my own happy childhood I realize more and more the wonderful sense of security and happiness which comes from a loved home.'

During the summer of 1948 the King's cramp in both legs had become worse. At Balmoral in August he was suffering discomfort most of the time. Sir Morton Smart who examined him, was gravely alarmed, and called in Sir Maurice Cassidy, the heart specialist.

The doctors found the King to be suffering from an obstruction to the circulation

Above:
Buckingham Palace floodlit to commemorate the wedding of Princess Elizabeth and the newly created Duke of Edinburgh in 1947.

Opposite:
Photograph commemorating the engagement of Princess Elizabeth and Lieutenant Philip Mountbatten R.N. in July 1947. With the Royal couple are the King, Queen and Princess Margaret.

through the arteries of the legs. There was a danger of gangrene developing and even that his right leg might have to be amputated. This news was kept from Princess Elizabeth, whose first child was almost due. Two days later, on 14th November, she gave birth to Prince Charles, the King and Queen's first grandchild. 'I wish so much that Alla had lived to see this', the Queen told her sister Lady Granville. For the first time the presence of the Home Secretary at the birth was dispensed with, as the survival of an archaic custom. The Queen had a busy time visiting her husband and daughter, both ensconced in different parts of Buckingham Palace!

A royal tour of Australia and New Zealand had long been projected, the first to have been undertaken by a King and Queen. It was therefore very distressing for him to have to postpone it indefinitely on his doctor's advice.

By December the danger of amputation passed, and the King and Queen spent Christmas at Sandringham, but on 3rd March there was more disquieting news. It fell to Professor Learmouth to break it to the King that he would have to undergo an operation, and to the Queen he said 'that the King should avoid much exertion. He may pay more heed to you Ma'am, than to his doctors'.

The operation was performed on 12th March. Early that morning, the Queen went with her daughters to Communion in the Chapel Royal, St. James's Palace. There was great public concern, and large crowds gathered outside the Palace. Relief came when newspaper bills carried the message: 'He's all right.' When Professor Learmonth's patient asked him for his dressing gown, he produced a sword from under his pillow. 'You used a knife on me', said the King, 'Now I'm going to use one on you.' There and then he bestowed a knighthood on the kneeling surgeon.

During 1950 the King's health improved. The Queen spent her fiftieth birthday, 4th

August, with him in London. As Princess Elizabeth was expecting her second baby, the King travelled north alone to fulfil some engagements. Eleven days later Princess Anne, a name denied by King George V to the King and Queen for their second daughter, Princess Margaret was born at Clarence House. 'How very nice to have another girl in the family!' commented the Queen.

The centenary of the Prince Consort's great Exhibition was marked in 1951 by the Festival of Britain, a brain-child of Herbert Morrison, known as 'Lord Festival'. On 3rd May the King and Queen went to St. Paul's Cathedral, and on the steps declared the Festival open, which was followed by a Service of dedication. The next day they toured the Exhibition on the South Bank which proved to be the King's last major public appearance. This was a busy time for them. In the following week, King Frederik and Queen Ingrid of Denmark came on a State Visit, and on the 24th the King installed the Duke of Gloucester as Great Master of the Order of the Bath. That afternoon he went on to the Imperial Institute but he was not feeling well and in the evening was ordered to bed.

The Queen carried out the duties of host to the aged King of Norway, King Haakon. She sat at his side at the Royal Banquet and took him to the Royal Tournament, where the massed bands played 'Here's a health unto His Majesty', but it was not to be.

In August the King and Queen went up to Balmoral, and here Princess Margaret celebrated her twenty-first birthday. Within a week he was back in London being X-rayed. He flew back on the following day, and on the 18th September was told that he would need to have part of his left lung removed. During that week the Queen left the Palace on only one occasion. The operation was performed there on Sunday 23rd September. That morning, she, her daughters and Prince Philip drove to the Chapel at Lambeth

The King and Queen attend the Sexcentenary Service of the Order of the Garter in St. George's Chapel, Windsor, held on St. George's Day, 1948.

Palace, where the Archbishop of Canterbury performed a special service to pray for the King's recovery.

At last the King felt better, and by the end of November he and the Queen went to Royal Lodge, Windsor, which was her first visit there for four months. On 9th December she joined in the National Thanksgiving for his recovery at the little Chapel of All Saints in Windsor Great Park. Two days later saw the fifteenth Anniversary of the Accession, and on the 14th, his fifty-sixth and last birthday. This was celebrated by a family luncheon party at Buckingham Palace, of which the guests included Queen Mary, the Duke of Gloucester and the Princess Royal.

For his last Christmas at Sandringham there was a family reunion. Princess Elizabeth and Prince Philip returned from touring Canada, and also Prince Charles and Princess Anne came to be with their grandparents. The King insisted on giving his customary broadcast, which for the first time was pre-recorded. The Queen sat helping him while he patiently went through the script again and again, often struggling for breath.

His husky voice shocked the nation, but his courage triumphed. 'Christmas is, and always will be, a time when we can and should count our blessings,' he said. 'The blessings of hope, the blessings of happy gatherings, and the blessing of the hopeful message of Christmas.'

Dr. Malan, the South African Prime Minister, had placed Botha House on the

South African coast at the disposal of the King and Queen, for him to recuperate in the warmth and sunshine. They were due to voyage out in H.M.S. *Vanguard* on 10th March 1952. Princess Elizabeth and Prince Philip undertook the much-postponed Australian and New Zealand tour on their behalf.

The King enjoyed New Year's Day 1952 shooting with Prince Philip and a few friends around Heath Farm. A few days later the Queen and Princess Elizabeth attended the Hurst Park Races. That January he felt much better, and told a member of the household, 'this just shows that an operation is not an illness – I am now all right'.

The whole family went to Drury Lane on 30th January to see 'South Pacific', to wish *bon voyage* to Princess Elizabeth and Prince Philip. The next morning the King, Queen and Princess Margaret went to see them off at Heathrow Airport on the first lap of their long round-the-world tour, an overnight flight to Nairobi.

The King stood hatless in the biting wind on the tarmac waving their plane goodbye. Oliver Lyttelton, in attendance wrote, 'I was shocked by the King's appearance … He seemed much altered and strained. I had the

Above:
In 1951 the King and Queen visit the Festival of Britain on the South Bank of London. It was his last major official programme.

Left: The Royal Family say goodbye to Princess Elizabeth as she leaves for her tour of Australia, New Zealand and Africa.

Opposite:
Princess Anne's christening in 1950, a photograph taken by Baron in the Drawing Room at Buckingham Palace.

101

THE ROYAL ANCESTRY OF HER MAJESTY QUEEN ELIZABETH THE QUEEN MOTHER

ROBERT II (STEWART) KING OF SCOTS 1371–1390 = ELIZABETH MURE

JEAN

SIR JOHN LYON of Glamis (d.1382)

SIR JOHN LYON of Glamis (d.1435) = ELIZABETH GRAHAM

PATRICK LYON, 1st LORD GLAMIS (d.1459) = ISOBEL OGILVY

JOHN LYON, 3rd LORD GLAMIS (d.1497) = ELIZABETH SCRYMGEOUR

JOHN LYON, 4th LORD GLAMIS (d.1500) = ELIZABETH GRAY da. of Lord Gray

JOHN LYON, 6th LORD GLAMIS (d.1528) = JANET DOUGLAS sister of Earl of Angus

JOHN LYON, 7th LORD GLAMIS (d.1559) = JANET KEITH sister of Earl Marischal

JOHN LYON, 8th LORD GLAMIS (killed 1578) = ELIZABETH ABERNETHY, da. of Lord Saltoun

PATRICK LYON, 1st EARL OF KINGHORNE (d.1615) = Lady ANNE MURRAY da. of Earl of Tullibardine

JOHN LYON, 2nd EARL OF KINGHORNE (d.1646) = Lady ELIZABETH MAULE, da. of Earl of Panmure

PATRICK LYON, 3rd EARL OF STRATHMORE AND KINGHORNE (d.1695) = Lady HELEN MIDDLETON, da. of Earl of Middleton (d.1708)

ELIZABETH OF YORK (d.1503) = HENRY VII (TUDOR) KING OF ENGLAND 1485–1509

CHARLES BRANDON, DUKE OF SUFFOLK (d.1545) = MARY, DOWAGER QUEEN OF FRANCE (d.1533)

HENRY GREY, DUKE OF SUFFOLK (executed 1554) = LADY FRANCES BRANDON (d.1559)

EDWARD SEYMOUR, EARL OF HERTFORD (d.1621) = LADY KATHERINE GREY (d.1568)

HONOR ROGERS (d.1615) = EDWARD SEYMOUR, LORD BEAUCHAMP (d.1612)

Lady FRANCES DEVEREUX da. of Earl of Essex (favourite of Elizabeth I) (d.1674) = WILLIAM SEYMOUR, 2nd DUKE OF SOMERSET (d.1660)

CHARLES BOYLE, VISCOUNT DUNGARVAN (d.1694) = Lady JANE SEYMOUR (d.1679)

JULIANA NOEL (d.1750) = CHARLES BOYLE, 3rd EARL OF CORK (d.1704)

Lady DOROTHY SAVILE (d.1758) = RICHARD BOYLE, 4th EARL OF CORK (d.1753)

WILLIAM CAVENDISH, 4th DUKE OF DEVONSHIRE (d.1764) = CHARLOTTE ELIZABETH BOYLE, BARONESS CLIFFORD OF LANESBOROUGH (d.1754)

JOHN LYON, 4th EARL OF STRATHMORE AND KINGHORNE (d.1712) = Lady ELIZABETH STANHOPE, da. of Earl of Chesterfield (d.1723)

THOMAS LYON, 8th EARL OF STRATHMORE AND KINGHORNE (d.1753) = JEAN NICHOLSON (d.1778)

JOHN LYON (later BOWES) 9th EARL OF STRATHMORE AND KINGHORNE (d.1776) = MARY ELEANOR BOWES (heiress of Streatlam Castle, Co. Durham d.1800)

THOMAS LYON-BOWES, 11th EARL OF STRATHMORE AND KINGHORNE (d.1846) = MARY ELIZABETH LOUISA RODNEY CARPENTER (d.1811)

THOMAS GEORGE LYON-BOWES, LORD GLAMIS (d.1834) = CHARLOTTE GRIMSTEAD (d.1881)

CLAUDE BOWES-LYON, 13th EARL OF STRATHMORE AND KINGHORNE (d.1904) = FRANCES DORA SMITH (d.1922)

CLAUDE GEORGE BOWES-LYON, 14th EARL OF STRATHMORE AND KINGHORNE (d.1944) = NINA CECILIA CAVENDISH-BENTINCK (d.1938)

WILLIAM HENRY CAVENDISH-BENTINCK, 3rd DUKE OF PORTLAND (d. 1809) = Lady DOROTHY CAVENDISH (d.1794)

Lord (WILLIAM) CHARLES AUGUSTUS CAVENDISH-BENTINCK (d.1826) = ANNE WELLESLEY, da. of Richard Wellesley Marquess Wellesley, brother of the great Duke of Wellington (d. 1875)

Rev. CHARLES WILLIAM FREDERICK CAVENDISH-BENTINCK (d.1865) = CAROLINE LOUISA BURNABY (later Mrs Henry Warren Scott, d.1918)

HER MAJESTY QUEEN ELIZABETH THE QUEEN MOTHER (b.1900) = HIS MAJESTY KING GEORGE VI (d.1952)

HER MAJESTY QUEEN ELIZABETH II (b.1926) = H.R.H. PRINCE PHILIP, DUKE OF EDINBURGH

H.R.H. PRINCESS MARGARET (b.1930) = ANTONY ARMSTRONG-JONES, EARL OF SNOWDON (div. 1978)

H.R.H. PRINCE CHARLES, PRINCE OF WALES (b.1948) = LADY DIANA SPENCER

H.R.H. PRINCESS ANNE (b.1950) = Captain MARK PHILLIPS

H.R.H. PRINCE ANDREW (b.1960)

H.R.H. PRINCE EDWARD (b.1964)

DAVID, VISCOUNT LINLEY, (b. 1961)

Lady SARAH ARMSTRONG-JONES (b.1964)

H.R.H. PRINCE WILLIAM OF WALES (b.1982)

H.R.H. PRINCE HENRY OF WALES (b.1984)

PETER PHILLIPS (b.1977)

ZARA PHILLIPS (b.1981)

feeling of doom, which grew as the minutes before the time of departure ebbed away. The King went on to the roof of the building to wave goodbye. The high wind blew his hair into disorder. I felt with deep foreboding that this would be the last time he was to see his daughter, and that he thought so himself.'

It was a sunny crisp day on 5th February. That morning before 10.00 a.m. the King went out to the Flitcham beat for some rough shooting on 'keepers' day. There were some twenty guns, including Michael Adeane, Lord Fermoy (grandfather to the Princess of Wales, as yet unborn), tenants and some visiting gamekeepers. For six hours the party tramped over the frosty fields, with only a break for a picnic lunch in the village hall, and bagged 280 hares, four rabbits and brought down two pigeons.

The Queen and Princess Margaret lunched at Ludham with Edward Seago, the artist, who afterwards took them by motor cruiser to Barton Broad, where they had tea at Barton Hall. They brought back with them Edward Seago's paintings of Sandringham, which they had commissioned.

At the end of the shoot the King told his friends, 'A good day's sport, gentlemen. I will expect you here at nine o'clock on Thursday'.

When the Queen returned they went into the Hall to look at Seago's pictures. At dinner there was much laughter; the King was in great form. By coincidence, one of their guests was a brother-in-law of Lady Bettie Walker who, with her husband, ran the Outspan Hotel at Nyeri, Kenya, and who had invited Princess Elizabeth and Prince Philip that very night to stay in their observation post, Treetops. Twice that evening the King walked over to the Kennels to see 'Roddy', his golden retriever, who had a thorn in his paw. Princess Margaret played on the piano, and after listening to the news about Princess Elizabeth's tour went to bed at 10.30. The Queen took the party down to the Ballroom to watch a film.

The King was quietly reading in bed when the footman took him his cup of cocoa. About midnight the nightwatchman saw him come to the window and fasten the catch.

At 7.30 in the morning, James MacDonald, the second valet, knocked at the King's door with his tray and went to run his bath. Not hearing the King's customary cough, the valet returned twenty minutes later. As the King seemed to be asleep he brought up a fresh tray. There was no movement. The valet went closer and saw that the King had died in his sleep. The bedclothes were not disturbed.

Captain Sir Harold Campbell, the Equerry, was informed and it fell to him to break the news to the Queen. She met the blow with the utmost courage and great self control. 'I never knew a woman could be so brave', said a member of the Household.

Meanwhile, Martin Charteris, Princess Elizabeth's Private Secretary, who was lunching at the Outspan Hotel in Kenya, received unconfirmed reports of the tragedy. After the news had come through officially, he told Commander Mike Parker, the Equerry, at Treetops, who in turn told Prince Philip. At 5.00 that evening on 6th February the grief-stricken Queen Elizabeth II started her long journey home from the nearest airfield Nanyuki.

Queen Elizabeth was now Her Majesty Queen Elizabeth The Queen Mother.

The Queen Mother

King George VI's early death at the age of fifty-six proved a shattering blow to Queen Elizabeth, but she bore her grief with all the fortitude that one would expect of her. On the day he died she came as usual to play with her grandchildren, Prince Charles and Princess Anne, with the remark 'I have got to start sometime, and it is better now than later'. But when Princess Marie Louise spoke of the bravery she showed, she replied, 'Not when I am alone'.

The new Queen, Elizabeth II, flew back from Kenya the day after her accession. An announcement was made that in future her mother would be known as 'Her Majesty Queen Elizabeth The Queen Mother'. To the Royal Household she is called briefly 'Queen Elizabeth' in distinction to 'the Queen' and this description is sometimes adopted in this book. She was the third Queen Consort of England to have been mother of a reigning Queen. The others were Catherine of Aragon mother of Mary I and Anne Boleyn mother of Elizabeth I.

Through this initial period of great sorrow and sadness, the Queen Mother was sustained by her family and close friends. 'Her daughters were wonderful during this dreadful time', said a friend. Sir Winston Churchill, once again Prime Minister and the first to serve the new Queen, gave her mother valued advice. 'That valiant woman', he called her. When in Scotland she did not ask visitors from Balmoral over to Birkhall, but Sir Winston did not wait to be invited. What he then said is unknown but it started her on a long road to recovery to a new life.

The Queen Mother never forgot the skill and devotion which the nursing staff from the Westminster Hospital gave to the King in his illness. She asked Sister Doreen Pearce and Sister Ruth Beswetherwick, when off duty, to come as her guests to the Royal Variety performance at the Victoria Palace. There was a thunderous applause from the audience when the two nurses in uniform entered the Royal box.

Birkhall, that sequestered little Georgian house in Deeside, seven miles from the much larger Balmoral, had been a wedding present from King George V and Queen Mary and was always a favourite home. The Duke and Duchess of York, as they then were, had planned the garden between them, much of it on a steep slope. Many members of the Royal Family spent part of their honeymoon there, including the Queen and Prince Philip, the Duke and Duchess of Kent and Princess Alexandra and the Hon. Angus Ogilvy. The Queen once called it 'the nicest place in the whole world'.

An equally loved home was Royal Lodge, Windsor, but her main house was Clarence House in London which she now exchanged with the Queen and Prince Philip, who moved into Buckingham Palace.

Clarence House is a square cream-painted house on the north side of The Mall, officially forming part of St. James's Palace. John Nash rebuilt it in 1828 for the Duke of Clarence, who later reigned as King William IV before his niece, Queen Victoria. For many years Clarence House was old-fashioned and shabby. In 1949 it was transformed for Princess Elizabeth and Prince Philip, and in the following year Princess Anne was born there.

The Queen Mother redecorated Clarence House with her own colour schemes and extended the amenities of the staff rooms. She was only able to move in two weeks before her daughter's Coronation. A pipe major of The London Scottish, a regiment of which she is Honorary Colonel, piped every morning before her window when she was in residence, but in recent years this has been

The south front of Clarence House. Built by the Duke of Clarence who later became William IV, it was the home of Princess Elizabeth and Prince Philip. After Princess Elizabeth became Queen in 1953, the Queen Mother moved there.

restricted to her birthdays and special occasions.

In the summer of 1952 the Queen Mother sought solace with her great friends Lady Doris Vyner and her husband Commander Vyner at their home the House of the Northern Gate, high above Dunnet Head on the picturesque coast of remote Caithness. They took her for several drives in the vicinity and on one of them they looked at the 400-year-old Barrogill Castle, lying 3.2 kilometres (2 miles) away, with magnificent views over the Orkneys. This was built by the 4th Earl of Caithness and was the home for many generations of the Sinclairs, Lairds and Barons of Mey.

This ancient Castle, standing only 366m (400yd) from the sea, looked desolate and forlorn but somehow defiant. The estate had been put up for sale by the then owner, Captain Imbert-Terry, but no offers had been forthcoming. The Queen Mother was told that its probable fate would be demolition. She was appalled and immediately became interested in its purchase. After travelling up a few times more, she finally made up her mind in August to buy the Castle. She thus became owner of one of the most northerly Castles on mainland Scotland, which she decided to call by its original name, the Castle of Mey. This is the only property which is really hers: the remainder are the Queen's, either as Crown property or privately owned.

Much work needed to be carried out. Storms had damaged the roof, and despite the outside walls being 2.74m (9ft) thick they were damp, as were the ceilings. At last, in 1955, her standard flew from the flagstaff of the Castle of Mey. She was in residence.

The turrets, winding stairs and the small rooms, particularly the Sitting Room, were reminiscent of the older parts of Glamis Castle. But now the Queen Mother had a well-heated, comfortable all-electric Castle of her own. 'Mey is tiny and enchanting, with a wonderful atmosphere of peace', said a visiting relative. 'It remains for Queen Elizabeth a haven from the world.' The Queen Mother also bought the adjoining 48.5hec (120ac) Longgoe Farm, where she has a herd of pedigree Angus cattle.

She delights in showing her little Castle to her friends. The distinguished traveller, Freya Stark, came to stay in 1975. The Queen Mother showed her the garden and took her down to the beach 'where she has a little seat that looks over the sea'.

The first public engagement Queen Elizabeth undertook after the King's death was in May 1952 at Crail in Fifeshire. As Colonel-in-Chief of The Black Watch she came to say goodbye to the first Battalion, on its way to Korea. She was dressed in deep black, as she continued for a whole year, matching the arm bands of the Officers of The Black Watch. She fulfilled every part of her programme, inspecting the Battalion, talking to many Officers, men and their relatives, as well as Old Comrades. She visited the Sergeants' Mess, was photographed with the Battalion, but in her short speech wishing them Godspeed, she did not trust herself to refer to the King.

It was also in May that the first passenger jet air liner, the Comet, flew on its inaugural flight to Johannesburg. The Queen Mother was lunching at Hatfield House with her friends, the Marquess and Marchioness of Salisbury a few days later, when Lord Salisbury mentioned that the trials were based on the De Havilland proving airfield nearby. He suggested, 'Why don't you try it, Ma'am?' She laughingly replied, 'You mean they have a Comet to spare?'

Lord Salisbury rang up Sir Miles Thomas, Chairman of BOAC, and shortly afterwards a select party climbed into a new Comet. This consisted of the Queen Mother, Princess Margaret, Group Captain Peter Townsend, Lord and Lady Salisbury, Sir Miles Thomas and the Queen Mother's two chauffeurs. They had a picnic lunch over the Alps flying at about 804kph (500mph) and then skirted the Mediterranean, before they touched down at Hatfield. In all they negotiated 2,977 kilometers (1,850 miles) in a four-hour flight.

At one point Her Majesty took the seat of the test pilot, John Cunningham, at the controls. She sent a radio message to her No. 600 Squadron of the Royal Auxiliary Air Force at Biggin Hill of which she is Honorary Air Commodore. 'I am delighted to tell you that today I took over as first pilot of the Comet Aircraft. We exceeded a reading of 0.8. mach. at 40,000 feet. What the passengers thought, I really would not like to say!'

Sir Miles Thomas later wrote of this flight: 'Her Majesty eased the control forward, the Comet gathered speed. Cunningham gave her a little extra throttle, the mach. needle crept towards the coloured danger sector and suddenly the Comet began to porpoise. Not violently, but just enough to indicate that we had reached the limits of her stability. Quickly, John eased the throttles back. Her Majesty did the same with the controls, and we went back to the same cruising speed as before the royal sprint. That trip was, of course, before the crashes that the Comet suffered through structural weakness, and had that porpoising gone on much longer, the wracking of the structure could well have precipitated a rupture of the skin of the kind that caused the subsequent tragedies. I still shudder every time I think of that flight.'

When King George VI died he was survived by three Queens: Queen Mary his mother, Queen Elizabeth his widow, and Queen Elizabeth II his daughter and successor. Soon only two remained. Queen Mary died aged eighty-five years on the afternoon of 24th March 1953, just over a month before her granddaughter's Coronation which she wanted so much to attend. Her last instructions were that the Coronation must not be delayed on account of her own death. 'She was the kindest and dearest mother-in-law', said the Queen Mother who was with her to the end.

Queen Elizabeth suffered another bereavement at this time. On 1st May 1953, her brother, Michael Bowes-Lyon, died four months before he reached his sixtieth birthday. It was Michael whom their brother David had refused to accept as dead all those years before, during the Great War.

On Coronation Day, 2nd June 1953, the Queen Mother took Prince Charles with her in the Glass Coach when she left Clarence House to see her daughter crowned as Queen Elizabeth II. Later, Princess Anne said, 'I was full of sisterly fury at being left behind', she was not yet three! Queen Elizabeth was only the second Queen Dowager to attend a Coronation following the precedent established by Queen Mary. She watched the magnificent ceremony from the middle of the

front row of the Royal Gallery. Cecil Beaton, in his diary, recalled that, 'even the towering height of the Mistress of the Robes [Mary, Duchess of Devonshire], was minimized by the enormous presence and radiance of the petite Queen Mother. Yet in the Queen widow's expression, we read sadness combined with pride.'

During the much delayed six months' Australian tour carried out by the Queen and Prince Philip, which started in the November of Coronation year, the Queen Mother took on many of her daughter's duties as the principal Counsellor of State. She held five investitures during which she conferred the accolade of knighthood upon Jacob Epstein, the sculptor, and George Robey, the comedian. Soon afterwards she was in Norway for

After buying the Castle of Mey in 1953, the Queen Mother was able to take up residence for the first time in October 1955. She here poses by an old cannon.

A formal group of the Queen, Prince Philip and their family in the Throne Room of Buckingham Palace after her Coronation in 1953.

the silver wedding celebrations of Crown Prince Olav and Princess Marthe.

Although the world did not know it until twelve days after the Coronation, something weighed heavily on Queen Elizabeth's mind. The news then broke that Princess Margaret wished to marry Group Captain Peter Townsend, the thirty-eight-year-old newly appointed Comptroller of her Household. In the previous December he had received the decree absolute as the innocent party in a divorce suit.

The Group Captain had a distinguished war record with the Royal Air Force and since 1944 had been with the King. He was his Equerry on that last trip to South Africa in H.M.S. *Vanguard* but no-one then suspected that he and the sixteen-year-old Princess would fall in love. He became Deputy

Master of the Household in 1950 and thus was always available, especially after the King's death had left a great void in the Princess's life.

The revelation placed the Queen, the Queen Mother and the Prime Minister Sir Winston Churchill, in a predicament. It was against the teaching of the Church of England to allow a marriage to be celebrated when a former spouse was still living.

There was one 'let out'. In the Royal Marriages Act of 1772 there is a clause that states, 'In case any descendant of George II, being above twenty-five years old, shall persist to contract a marriage disapproved of by the King, such descendant, after giving twelve months' notice to the Privy Council may contract such marriage and the same may be duly solemnized without the consent

no,' she said, 'I am perfectly all right,' but Princess Margaret caught 'Bulawayo 'flu' with a temperature of 103°, resulting in her return to Salisbury.

When in October 1955 the two years were up Group Captain Townsend returned to England. Both he and the Princess were constantly harried by the press, rising to a momentum when they were both weekend guests of Major and Mrs. Wills (a niece of the Queen Mother) at their home, Allanbury Park, Berkshire. The Prime Minister, Sir Anthony Eden, travelled to Balmoral to inform the Queen and Princess Margaret that the Cabinet would not consent to the marriage.

Princess Margaret returned to London and issued a statement from Buckingham Palace. 'I would like it to be known that I have decided not to marry Group Captain Townsend. I have been aware that it might be possible to contract a civil marriage. But mindful of the Church's teaching that Christian marriage is indissoluble and conscious of my duty to the Commonwealth, I have resolved to put these considerations before any others.' Any similarity with King Edward VIII's problems then ceased. Princess Margaret made her sacrifice, placing duty above personal happiness. Her religious beliefs and sense of duty triumphed in her case.

In November 1952 a fund had been launched in the United States to commemorate the late King, which was organized by Lewis Douglas, the American Ambassador, and supported by President Eisenhower. The money was to be spent providing technical training for young people from the Commonwealth in the United States. When the fund closed the sponsors invited the Queen Mother to come across to receive the cheque. Her twenty-three day visit to the United States in October and November 1954 proved a triumph, equalled only by her earlier tour with the King.

The Queen Mother sailed in H.M.S. *Queen Elizabeth* which she had launched in 1938, with her lady-in-waiting, Lady Jean Rankin. The presentation of the cheque was made at a banquet at the Waldorf-Astoria, then said to have been the largest, tallest and most expensive hotel in the world. Wearing evening dress sparkling with jewels, the Queen Mother found herself at dinner on a raised dais being televised to a wide network of viewers. The glaring lights and suffocating heat resulted in her toying with her food, duly noticed by Lady Jean.

of the King, and shall be good, except both Houses of Parliament shall declare their disapprobation thereof.'

Sir Winston therefore advised that Group Captain Townsend should be transferred abroad for two years. He was sent as Air Attaché to Brussels. This would allow Princess Margaret to reach the age of twenty-five before a final decision need be taken.

In the meantime the Queen Mother and Princess Margaret flew off by Comet to Southern Rhodesia, now Zimbabwe, on a sixteen day visit, with fifty four engagements to fulfil, the highlight being the opening of the Rhodes Centenary Exhibition at Bulawayo. Her Comet was the first jet aircraft to land at Salisbury, now Harare. It was bitterly cold. Queen Elizabeth, wearing a thin silk dress, was asked if she was frozen. 'Oh,

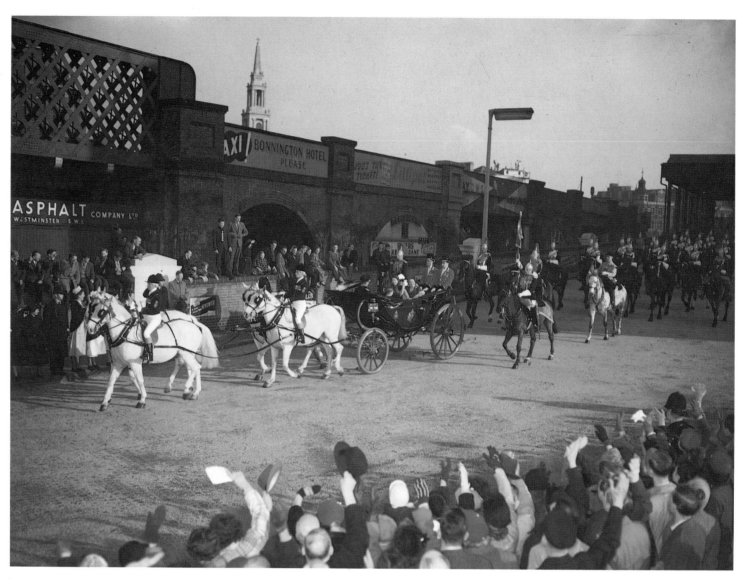

On returning from her
tour of North America in
1954, the Queen Mother
is accompanied in a
carriage by the Queen,
Prince Philip and Prince
Charles.

On returning to the home of Sir Pierson and Lady Dixon where they were staying, her hostess asked if she would like any refreshment. The Queen Mother hesitated, and then asked if it would be possible to have something like scrambled eggs 'but only if it would be no trouble'. She thoroughly enjoyed her supper on a tray in the drawing room, taking off her tiara and placing it on the sofa.

One of the most unlikely royal fans was John McGovern, the left-wing Labour M.P. for Shettleston, Glasgow, who had been imprisoned twice for campaigning against unemployment and had led hunger marches. He was at the Waldorf-Astoria banquet and wrote, 'royal personages were "untouchables" to me, (but) my wife and I had a splendid evening and cheered the Queen Mother heartily. I completely lost my proletarian snobbery. It was amazing that it had to be on American soil that I first recognized royalty.'

The Queen Mother went to see the *Pajama Game* and afterwards drank champagne with the caste. At a Pilgrim's luncheon she unveiled Frank Salisbury's painting of King George VI opening the Festival of Britain. She also went shopping and bought toys for her grandchildren, a magnetic bottle opener and a game of 'Scrabble' for herself.

She wanted to visit Sak's department store which was then holding an exhibition of jewellery, but word leaked out of her impending arrival. 'We shot up and down the lift just like a Marx Brothers' film, trying to find a floor where there was not a crowd waiting. Eventually we managed to get out at some improbable floor, but after a little while were were traced again', her lady-in-waiting said. The manager eventually took them to a boutique off the main hall where things were brought to her but the main object of seeing the store in action was not achieved.

In Washington the Queen Mother stayed at the White House with President and Mrs. Eisenhower and with Mamie she visited the famous Smithsonian Institution and the Mellon Art Gallery. She also went to Richmond, Virginia, and saw Williamsburg, whose colonial history had been re-created as a showpiece. The great welcome extended to her was summed up in the *New York Times* on the day of her arrival, 'Of all the many reasons for welcoming Queen Elizabeth the Queen Mother, the pleasantest is that she is so nice.'

After the United States, she spent a few days in Canada. It was on this trip that a move was made for her to become the next Governor-General. The Queen is reputed to have said to the proposal, 'I am afraid we could not spare her'.

In 1955, Queen Elizabeth became the first woman to fill the office of Chancellor of the University of London, Britain's largest university. This was no sinecure and she regularly attended all sorts of university occasions, which amounted to at least ten a year. There were Foundation Day ceremonies when Honorary Degrees are presented at Senate House and twice-yearly Presentation Days at the Royal Albert Hall. In her academic robes of black and gold she delivered her 'charge (or speech) to the Graduates,' and then 'hooded' all graduates – bachelors and those receiving higher degrees. This ceremony takes at least two hours to complete.

It was the prerogative of the President of the Students' Union to be the first partner to dance with the Chancellor of the University. Godfrey Talbot tells an amusing story about a nervous young President taking the floor with her radiant Majesty who smiled as she avoided the heavier kicks on the ankles. Such was her skill that he thought he was doing better than he had imagined. 'It was, however, a rough ride as the two twirled and bumped along – but a dance which made the boy (who is now a Q.C. and M.P.) a Queen Mum worshipper ever since, for in the middle of it all Her Majesty murmured into his ear: "Don't worry, Mr. President. You haven't knocked my tiara off – yet".'

The Queen Mother's tiara had a special significance in the University of London. When she arrived there on Foundation Day after attending some important function where tiaras were worn, she handed this to the Vice-Chancellor who in turn deputed a Fellow to place it carefully in a safe. Once, when he opened the safe and attempted to slide the tiara in, the door banged shut, snapping the tiara in two.

Normally, Chancellors of Universities retire at the age of seventy-five, but the Queen Mother was implored to stay on. She agreed, though the growing numbers of undergraduates meant that she was unable to continue 'hooding' everyone. When she did retire at eighty later in 1980, her granddaughter Princess Anne was elected the next Chancellor.

In April 1956 the Queen Mother had her first flight in a helicopter from Windsor to Biggin Hill, becoming the first member of the Royal Family to do so. She said that the 'chopper' transformed her life, 'as it did that of Anne Boleyn'. She beat Prince Philip, who was also 'chopper minded', to become the first to fly by helicopter from Sandringham to Buckingham Palace.

She visited France that year, once again renewing her acquaintanceship with a country she loved. She opened the Franco-Scottish Exhibition at the Hotel de Rohan in Paris, when in her speech in French, she referred to her Scottish and French forebears, 'I am sure the thistle of Scotland is flourishing still among the roses of France'.

She was back in France in June 1957 to unveil the Dunkirk Memorial to the 4,500 men who died on the beaches. She sailed with the Duke of Gloucester on the destroyer H.M.S. *Chieftain*. The little ships were not forgotten. Fifty cabin cruisers and other light river craft from the Thames took part in the ceremony. Among them was the motor yacht *Sundowner*; aboard was Mrs. Sylvia Lightoller, whose late husband sailed from Twick-

The Queen Mother being installed as the first Royal Chancellor of the University of London at a ceremony held at the Royal Festival Hall in 1955.

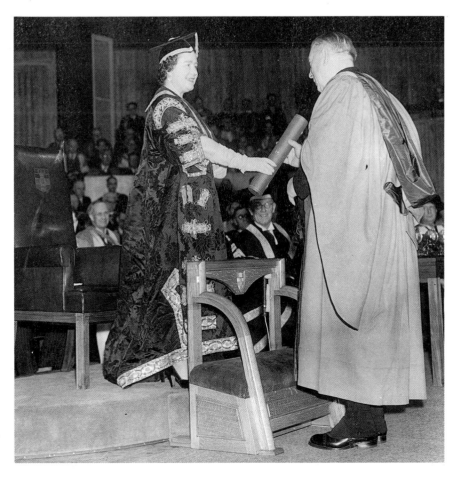

enham with their son to rescue 130 men from the sinking destroyer *Worcester*.

As H.M.S. *Chieftain* returned towards Dover, the Queen Mother's wreath of laurel and roses was slowly lowered over the side in a final tribute to the gallant men who did not return from Dunkirk.

Queen Elizabeth's most extensive tour was to New Zealand and Australia beginning in January 1958 when for the first time a member of the Royal Family flew around the world. She had only just recovered from influenza and despite the strain of travel fatigue flew out direct to Auckland, touching down at Montreal, Vancouver, Honolulu and Fiji. At Vancouver she confessed to being 'very tired, but so glad to be here'. When in Fiji, in a native *bure* (or thatched cottage) she went to the bathroom. Her lady-in-waiting heard her gasp and on rushing in, found a gigantic frog, glaring and winking at the Queen Mother.

On her last visit to Fiji the King had protected her from tasting the national drink of *yaqona* (*kava* to other Polynesian groups), an exceedingly bitter fluid made from roots. This time she bravely swallowed most of the draught from the ceremonial cup and looked at the Governor, Sir Ronald Garvey, with a smile of triumph. But he shook his head. She then drained every bitter drop from the cup when the great shout went up: 'it is empty'.

In Wellington, New Zealand, the weather was boiling. In the garden of Government House the Queen Mother sat with the towering Queen Salote of Tonga who made such a hit at the Coronation. They laughed and joked and had one fan between them which they shared. Long afterwards Queen Salote could talk of nothing else but her charm and sense of humour. At the races the Queen Mother was presented with a four-year-old gelding, 'Bali Hai', who turned out to be one of the winners. Mr. Holyoake, the New Zealand Prime Minister, could not find praise enough for the royal visitor, 'It's tremendous, she's terrific . . .'.

The tour in Australia was originally intended to cover the eastern states only, but was extended to include South and Western Australia. In Sydney during a particularly hot day the Queen Mother unveiled a plaque in the Mother and Infant Welfare building, still unfinished, in the grounds of Sydney University. She walked over the rough concrete floor to chat to the building foreman who wore an open-necked shirt and told him that he was much more suitably clad than the official guests perspiring in their morning dress.

Having a free Sunday in Melbourne, she asked that a dinner party should be arranged to meet 'the young marrieds' as this was a group she did not meet as much as she would like.

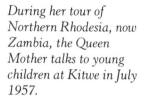

During her tour of Northern Rhodesia, now Zambia, the Queen Mother talks to young children at Kitwe in July 1957.

Above:
The Queen Mother in
conversation outside
Government House,
Canberra, during her
1958 tour of Australia.

Left:
During her tour of
Australia in 1958, the
Queen Mother puts out
her hand to call a
nondescript dog that
dashed on to the Royal
dais at the unveiling of a
plaque at Sydney
University.

115

At Melbourne University there was tight security to prevent the undergraduates becoming out of hand. This did not go unnoticed. The Queen Mother commented that 'it is a pity that they are so quiet. Unless they reach an uncomfortable stage, a students' rag is fun'. She added, as an afterthought, 'though flour bombs are a little uncomfortable of course'.

After a successful tour she flew off from Perth on 7th March on board a QANTAS airliner but when 322 kilometres (200 miles) from Mauritius, on her way to open the Embakasi Airport at Nairobi, Kenya, a cylinder cracked in one of the engines and several cowling pieces were broken open. The air-

In 1959 Queen Elizabeth visits the new Treetops Hotel in Kenya, the old one where her daughter became Queen had been destroyed by Mau Mau terrorists.

craft had to fly on three engines to Mauritius. 'This is the second time I have had trouble getting here', the Queen Mother told the people, referring to the fire in H.M.S. *Renown* in 1927.

A new engine cowling was placed on board another aircraft in Australia, but this unfortunately ran into a cyclone and was grounded in the Cocos Islands. The Queen Mother, instead of touching down for a short visit to Mauritius as planned, stayed with the Governor during the delay for two whole days. She told the Governor of Kenya that she was distressed at not being able to open the airport, but 'on another voyage, which I hope will not be too far in the future, my aircraft will land at your Airport'.

When the relief plane arrived in Mauritius, the engineers had to work in torrential rain from the tail-end of the cyclone to install the new engine. Then at Entebbe another fault developed, this time in the ignition of the replacement engine, probably due to the cyclone. Those working let flow some strong language when they were startled to find the Queen Mother standing by them. 'She was not fazed [worried] in the slightest', they said, and her sympathy and her remarkable technical knowledge of what they were trying to do, 'gave them an immense lift'.

A Britannia aircraft stood by at Nairobi, but it was Queen Elizabeth's express wish that the Australian aircraft should take her back to London. This was thwarted by a further blow in Malta, when another delay occurred due to hydraulic trouble. She then reluctantly agreed to transfer to a Britannia aircraft of BOAC. She sent a message to QANTAS, 'It could have happened to anyone. I feel sorry for the crew: they worked so hard'. She returned to London nearly three days late.

A year later, in February 1959 the Queen Mother made her promised visit to Kenya. She spent a night at the Treetops Hotel but not in the same observation lodge where her daughter had become Queen. This had been burned down by the Mau Mau and a similar one erected nearby. Her party, including her two ladies-in-waiting, Lady Hambleden and Lady Jean Rankin, watched some rhino, buffalo and baboon from the observation platform. Her Majesty remarked, 'The last time I was in Kenya in 1925 I saw a number of rhino from ground-level and was not too fond of them. I feel much happier seeing them from this platform.'

It was inaccurately reported in the *Natal*

Daily News a year later that the Queen Mother had been bitten on the arm by a baboon she was feeding when distracted by the arrival of a pair of rhino. It is true that she had a tiny piece of plaster on her arm, but this covered only the bite of a fly!

As the hot sun beat down on Narok, the tribal capital of the Masai, Queen Elizabeth told the vast gathering, 'I hope you will be blessed with good rains'. A few minutes later a loud crack of thunder gave way to a downpour. The Masai warriors leaped for joy, carrying their shields above their heads, and the womenfolk danced and chanted. Her reputation as a 'rainmaker' was established.

April 1959 saw the Queen Mother with Princess Margaret visiting Rome. She visited the Villa d'Este, and the Princess explored some of the churches. They both had an audience with Pope John XXIII at the Vatican. They stayed with the Marchese Incisa della Rochetta to see his stud farm at Ol-

giante near Rome and particularly 'Ribot' who in 1956 had beaten the Queen's horse 'High Veldt' at Ascot. In Paris they lunched with President de Gaulle at the Elysée Palace, and one day the Queen Mother drove out to the Forest of Fontainebleau to lunch with the Marquis de Ganay at the Château de Cour-ances (he was one of those who appeared in Robert Lacey's television series, *Aristocrats* in 1983).

On 19th February 1960 the Queen gave birth to her second son and third child, Prince Andrew, to the great delight of his grandmother the Queen Mother. He was the first child of a reigning monarch to be born for 103 years, in fact since Queen Victoria's youngest daughter, Princess Beatrice. When the Prince was three weeks old the Queen Mother received a present for him at a crafts exhibition held in the Victoria and Albert Museum, a velvet patchwork ball. 'He looks as if he could kick it around now', she said.

After an audience with Pope John XXIII in April 1959, the Queen Mother and Princess Margaret leave the Vatican.

He was an extrovert from the very start!

Just before Prince Andrew was born the Queen gave her consent to the engagement of Princess Margaret and a leading society photographer, Antony Armstrong-Jones, which was announced a week later. No one could have been more pleased than the Queen Mother. The announcement in the press on 26th February was for once the first intimation that they had of the engagement and they scurried to write up all the background story.

Princess Margaret married Antony Armstrong-Jones at Westminster Abbey on 6th May. In October of the following year the bridegroom accepted from the Queen an earldom, choosing to be Earl of Snowdon, with Viscount Linley for his son's courtesy title. David, Viscount Linley, the Queen Mother's fourth grandson, was born a month later.

It is remarkable also that the press did not discover another long-standing secret. Tony Armstrong-Jones rented a room from his friend William Glenton at 59 Rotherhithe Street, S.E.16, overlooking the River Thames in London's dockland. This hideout for the couple continued for nearly four years after the wedding and they remained undetected.

The only disguises were her headscarf and their dark glasses. 'I think this is one of the sweetest rooms I know. It's made us so happy', Princess Margaret said.

Bill Glenton tells the remarkable story in *Tony's Room*. In 1962 the Queen Mother came to Rotherhithe. On this occasion glasses clinked, the sound of the piano broke out as Margaret played a mixture of old and new popular tunes, with the Queen Mother singing as gaily as the rest. Tony cooked the meal, with less-powerful cooking smells coming through the floorboards than usual. The swans on the river congregated to receive crumbs thrown by the Queen Mother. After midnight the singing faded after a lusty rendering of *La Marseillaise* as a French freighter (or so they thought) passed slowly by.

On leaving 'Tony's Room' the Queen Mother stopped her car to wander in St. Mary's Churchyard to look for the graves of some of the Mayflower's crew. She said she had not enjoyed an evening so much since she was a girl of twenty.

Usually the Queen distributes the Royal Maundy on Maundy Thursday, the day before Good Friday, but the Queen Mother has twice done so, in 1960 and 1970, both

Group taken after the wedding of Princess Margaret and Antony Armstrong-Jones in 1960 by Cecil Beaton in the Throne Room at Buckingham Palace. The Queen Mother stands next to the bride.

times at Westminster Abbey. Carrying her posy of flowers and sweet-smelling herbs she distributed the specially minted Maundy Money to the same number of men and women as the Sovereign has years. Generally, the recipients' age is about eighty years. According to the Sub-Dean, over a cup of tea afterwards the Queen Mother is said to have remarked, 'I had no idea the service was so long.'

Another occasional visit is to the Chelsea Pensioners at the Royal Hospital Chelsea. Charles II planned the Hospital for old war pensioners but he died before it was opened in 1692. Founder's Day parade takes place on the nearest Thursday to 29th May, Charles II's birthday or Oakapple Day, in memory of his hiding in the oak tree in 1651 from Cromwell's Army.

The Queen Mother first took the parade on Founder's Day in 1966. After the inspection comes the March Past, with the Guards' band playing 'Boys of the Old Brigade'. Three cheers are called 'for our pious founder' and three cheers for the Sovereign.

Great personal sorrow befell the Queen Mother in 1961 with two family bereavements. In February her elder sister Mary (known in family circles as May) died, and in September Sir David Bowes-Lyon, four months under the age of sixty, with whom she had so close an affinity. He suffered badly from asthma. Her Majesty had invited him and his wife Rachel to Birkhall to have the benefit of the pure air of the Highlands when he unexpectedly had a heart attack.

In April 1961 Queen Elizabeth accepted an invitation from President Bourguiba of

Queen Elizabeth leaves Westminster Abbey after distributing the Royal Maundy in 1970.

Tunisia to visit his country and sailed in the Royal Yacht, H.M.S. *Britannia* from Portsmouth. She took her last surviving sister, Rose, Lady Granville, with her to rest on board. Another guest was Brigadier Bernard Fergusson (later Governor-General of New Zealand and Lord Ballantrae), who once commanded the 1st Battalion of The Black Watch.

It was her first visit to North West Africa, and Tunisia where her husband had come in 1943 to celebrate the Eighth Army's victories. She went to the heights of Takroma where so many brave young New Zealanders had fallen before its capture. The Royal party sailed on to Cagliari, Sardinia, to rendezvous with the Queen and Prince Philip. After their reunion the Queen took over the Royal Yacht to make a state visit to Italy, and the Queen Mother with her party returned to London by Comet.

In June the wedding took place in York Minster of her nephew, the Duke of Kent to Katharine Worsley. This the Queen Mother said was one of the nicest she could recall. As an example of her busy schedule she left Clarence House at 10.00 a.m. travelling by train from King's Cross. Straight after the wedding reception at Hovingham she flew to Heathrow, where she took the four-minute helicopter flight back to the Palace. Then she attended a Royal Gala Perfomance at Covent Garden at 9.00 p.m., returning to Clarence House well after midnight.

Despite breaking a small bone in her foot after an accident at Royal Lodge, she did not cancel any of her engagements. Her Majesty arrived in a wheel-chair to launch the liner *Northern Star* at Vickers-Armstrong's shipyard on Tyneside, where she was wheeled on to the launching platform. Her remarkable stamina can be seen when only a few days later she even dispensed with the wheel-chair at a reception at Lancaster House. This was given to 200 American teachers under a Government Exchange scheme. She limped across the lawn with her foot in bandages and sat resting her leg on a stool to shake the hands of all her guests for well over an hour.

In 1962 the Queen Mother was back in Canada. Once more royal history was made, this time by her travelling on an ordinary scheduled flight of a commercial aircraft with fee-paying passengers. The Black Watch of Canada (Royal Highland Regiment) was celebrating its centenary and welcomed their Colonel-in-Chief. At a spectacular ceremony held at McGill University she presented new colours to the Regiment.

Three months later she was back in Perth, celebrating her silver jubilee as Colonel-in-Chief of The Black Watch. Among the parade of 1,500 officers and men were veterans of the South African war, the two World Wars, and Korea. Unfortunately in the midst of the parade came a downpour.

The Queen Mother was frequently reproached by her Household when she was planning her tours abroad with heavy schedules: 'you never travel to please yourself'. At length in 1963, as a result of a conversation with her friend Sir Pierson Dixon, then Ambassador to France, a chance came. She was to visit the lovely Loire Valley and see the impressive châteaux. (This proved to be the first of six private holidays to France in that decade.)

Her Majesty took the first floor for a party of fifteen at the Château du Puits d'Artigny, near Montbazon, which had been converted into a hotel. Among the many châteaux she toured were the sixteenth-century Château of

The Queen Mother at the Chelsea Pensioners Founder's Day Parade at the Royal Hospital, Chelsea. She is talking to R/Sergeant Henry James Smith of Walsall, aged 93, and two of his comrades.

Above:
The Queen Mother takes her seat in the Royal Box at a Gala Performance at the Royal Opera House, Covent Garden in May 1963.

Left:
The Queen Mother in 1961 meets overseas students at a reception of the Y.W.C.A. in London of which she is Patron.

The first published photograph of Prince Andrew taken on his grandmother's sixtieth birthday, with Prince Charles and Princess Anne, August 1960.

Cheverny where she lunched with the Marquis and Marquise de Vibraye, and the moated Chenonçeau, where Mary Queen of Scots once stayed. She also travelled to the Abbey of Fontevraud to look at the tombs of her royal forebears, King Henry II and King Richard Lionheart. A distinguished Frenchman, Vicomte de Noailles, took charge of all the arrangements. On her last evening she went to a country restaurant famed for its local dishes.

A later visit was to the little fifteenth-century Château Legier near Arles in Provence, which she rented, taking a party of seven. She is always in tune with the people of France, having inherited French blood

from both sides of her family: Laujol of Montpellier, de Court, de Massue (Seigneurs de St. Aubyn-en-Rovière), de Bellangreville (Seigneurs de Fresnoye), and d'Ailly (Seigneurs de Pierrepont), to name but a few.

From the Loire Queen Elizabeth flew home for a Royal Wedding at Westminster Abbey in April 1963. Her niece, Princess Alexandra, daughter of the late Duke of Kent, was marrying the Hon. Angus Ogilvy, son of her Lord Chamberlain the Earl of Airlie. Angus's proposal of marriage was made to this happy bride in the garden of Birkhall during a house party. It was Princess Alexandra's birth on Christmas Day that was the one happy event of hat awful Abdication Year of 1936.

In 1964, there were four royal births in as many months. Not since the death of the Prince Regent's only child, Princess Charlotte in 1818 when her royal uncles, including Queen Victoria's father, put away their mistresses to marry princesses and enter the 'Royal baby stakes', had there been such a crop of royal infants.

The first to appear was in February when Princess Alexandra gave birth to her first child, James Ogilvy, on Leap Year Day. Then came the Queen's third son, Prince Edward, born on 3rd March. The Duchess of Kent's daughter, Lady Helen Windsor, was born on 28th April, and finally, on 1st May, came Princess Margaret's second child, Lady Sarah Armstrong-Jones. The Queen Mother's grandchildren now amounted to six, three sons and a daughter of the Queen and Prince Philip, and a son and a daughter of Princess Margaret and Lord Snowdon.

The next major tour was scheduled to take place in February 1964 but a week before the Queen Mother was due to set out on her 48,000-kilometre (30,000-mile) trip to Canada, Australia and New Zealand, she suddenly developed appendicitis, and on 3rd February was taken to King Edward VII Hospital for Officers, in London (known as 'Sister Agnes's), for an operation to remove the appendix. She was a model patient and within two weeks was back at Clarence House.

After a few weeks convalescing at Royal Lodge with Princess Margaret and her husband she flew to Kingston, Jamaica, to join the Royal Yacht *Britannia* for a three-weeks' cruise in the Caribbean to complete her recovery, but not without first seeing her new baby grandson, Prince Edward, at Buckingham Palace.

In November 1966 the Queen Mother visited the stars after the Royal Variety Performance at the London Palladium and is amused by Eric Morecambe and Ernie Wise off-stage.

When in Jamaica in February of the following year, that grand old lady, Princess Alice, Countess of Athlone, who had been for many years Chancellor of the University of the West Indies conferred upon the Queen Mother the honorary degree of Doctor of Letters. The Princess used to travel out by banana boat, usually with only one maid.

When the Queen Mother was in Jamaica she went for luncheon with her long-standing friend, Nöel Coward. He planned to give her curry in coconuts, fish mousse, rum cream pie and strawberries, but just before her arrival he had to make an iced soup because the fish mousse collapsed into a grey heap. 'As for me', he wrote in his diary, 'I am at her feet. She has infinite grace of mind, charm, humour and deep-down kindness, in addition to which she looks enchanting. She puts everyone at their ease immediately without condescension or apparent effort. She did me the honour of driving nearly eighty miles off her course to come and see me and I do really believe she enjoyed it.'

In early August Nöel Coward was invited by the Queen Mother to Sandringham during the King's Lynn Festival. This was organized by her friend and lady-in-waiting, Ruth, Lady Fermoy, and she goes year after year to enjoy its programme. This time Nöel Coward accompanied her to a church there to hear Rostropovitch, the Russian cellist. His diary states that 'after dinner at Sandringham ... I shall always cherish the memory of the Queen Mother and me singing as a duet, "My Old Man Said Follow the Van".'

There is an obverse side to the Queen Mother although she rarely shows it. Lady Longford quotes Lord David Cecil as saying, 'For someone so unaggressive she has a very strong personality ... She *could* be formidable'. He adds, 'I have never seen it'. The same was said of her mother, Lady Strathmore. A young friend of Princess Margaret was staying with Her Majesty and she asked him why he had not attended church. 'Oh, I usually lie in bed on Sunday mornings', he told her and was gently frozen out.

The postponed visit to Australia and New Zealand started in March 1966. On the day after the Queen Mother's arrival she spoke on the telephone to her seventeen-year-old grandson, Prince Charles. He had arrived at Timbertop, the bush annexe of Geelong Grammar School, three months earlier and she became his first visitor. 'I do believe you have grown a bit!' she said.

A week later Queen and Prince went on a fishing trip in the Snowy Mountains, staying in a cottage at River Bend. Both were very keen. She had taught him to fly fish in Scotland. During their time there the two had a narrow escape. When they were driving to see the Jindabyne hydro-electric dam on the Snowy River, their Rolls was suddenly forced off the road to avoid a head-on collision. In the other car was a honeymoon couple and they had been so busily looking at the Queen Mother that the driver crossed to the wrong side of the road.

The Queen Mother stayed with Princess Alice's daughter, Lady May and her husband Sir Henry Abel Smith, Governor of Queensland, and after leaving Australia spent Easter in Fiji. The Royal yacht *Britannia* took her on to New Zealand where she landed at the most southerly port of Bluff. This visit was more informal and she hoped for some good fishing, remembering that in 1927 she had caught twenty schnapper and a 3.6kg (8lb) trout. In fact, she fished for two days without a bite, postponing her dinner for another attempt. She then returned with a 0.90kg (2lb) rainbow trout and was heard to say, 'it would have been better to get one out of the deep-freeze. I hope to get bigger ones tomorrow'. But it was not to be.

On looking through her engagements she noticed an important omission. She had been presented with a horse 'Bali Hai', a flat-racer on a previous visit to New Zealand, and it had won for her the 1959 Queen Alexandra Stakes at Ascot. He was now in retirement. 'She is really awfully fond of him', said Sir Martin Gilliat, her Private Secretary, 'and has particularly asked that we try to arrange to visit him as soon as we reach Auckland.'

The Royal party had a short stop at Honolulu. The Queen Mother pleased onlookers by dancing the Hula with Hawaii's Duke Kahanamoku at the reception given in her honour by the Governor of Hawaii.

In September 1966 she launched Britain's first Polaris Submarine, H.M.S. *Resolution* at Barrow-in-Furness. On the afternoon of 6th December she attended a reception at St. James's Palace given by the Women's Voluntary Service. That evening she was admitted to the King Edward VII Hospital for Officers. On examination it was found that a serious abdominal operation was necessary for a partial obstruction. This was carried out by a team of six surgeons on the morning of 10th December, thirty years to the day when King Edward VIII signed his Instrument of Abdication. The bulletin said that she was

comfortable, though she commented that there is all the difference in the patient's meaning of the word and the surgeon's'.

The Queen Mother had to remain in hospital over Christmas and the New Year. Telegrams, letters, flowers and gifts swamped both Clarence House and the hospital and though there was a certain amount of disquiet among the public at the lack of precise information, they were reassured by the news that she was sitting up, well bandaged, watching her horse 'Irish Rover' win a race at Sandown Park.

The public first saw the Queen Mother at Sandringham three weeks later when she attended morning service at Flitcham Church nearby with the Queen and other members of the Royal Family.

She had no intention of letting up after her operation except for one or two strenuous duties. Among these was her appointment in the following year as Lord High Commissioner to the General Assembly of the Church of Scotland. This was particularly frustrating for her as it was an office the King had filled almost forty years earlier.

Four months after her operation she visited the West Country, and then sailed in the Royal Yacht *Britannia* to Normandy to be present at the twenty-third anniversary of the D-Day landings. The Mayor of Gray, near Arromanches, presented her with a photograph of the King, which had been taken on his arrival shortly after the landings.

Three deaths occurred in 1967 which caused the Queen Mother distress. Her two sisters-in-law, the Princess Royal, who had been a close friend ever since the Great War, and Princess Marina, Duchess of Kent, both died suddenly. Also, Queen Elizabeth's last

The Queen Mother relaxing during her 1966 tour of New Zealand by fishing for trout in Lake Wanaka, one of her favourite sports.

125

Above:
*A visit to the Royal
Smithfield Show in 1964
when the Queen Mother
admires a prize Aberdeen
Angus bull.*

Opposite:
*At the 1969 Braemar
Gathering the Queen
Mother attends with
Princess Anne, the Prince
of Wales, Princess
Margaret and her two
children.*

surviving sister Rose, Countess Granville died in a Forfar hospital at the age of seventy-seven, leaving her the last of her generation.

An unusual centenary celebrated in 1968 was that of the Central Markets, Smithfield, the centre of London's wholesale meat trade. It was arranged for the Queen Mother to walk through the market lanes and talk to the men at work. An official was warned, 'Mind you keep Her Majesty moving along' but he found his task more than difficult! She stopped first to chat with one group, then another, and was soon running late. When he pointedly took out his watch she noticed and said, 'Am I behind time?' 'Perhaps a little, Your Majesty.' 'Well', she answered, 'do tap your foot when you *know* I am.'

The men work on a shift system at Smithfield and when off-duty frequent the pubs and little cafés around the market, often singing old cockney songs. Here Hughie who played an accordion was a popular man, and on the occasion of the Royal visitor played

the Great War song, 'If you were the only Girl in the World and I was the only Boy'. The group took up this refrain and the Queen Mother, oblivious to time, said, 'I *must* listen to this'. One of the men commented that, 'she had tears in her eyes at the end. I think she was very touched by it. Suddenly we realized we were singing to the Queen Mother.'

During 1967 the Queen Mother was installed as the first Chancellor of the University of Dundee and regularly attended all their major occasions until she retired ten years later. In October 1968 she installed Peter Ustinov as Rector, who recalled that they were greeted with showers of toilet rolls! These were gracefully picked up by the Queen Mother much as if they were letters delivered to the wrong address.

There was a party to celebrate the British Equestrian Team's winning four gold medals in 1968 at the Olympic Games held in Mexico and the Queen Mother was invited as the guest of honour. She took along Princess

Right:
The Queen Mother
inspects a guard of honour
of Canadian ex-
servicemen at a service
held at Westminster
Abbey in 1967 to
celebrate Canada's
Centennial Year.

Below:
A seventieth-birthday
scene of the Queen
Mother with three of her
grandchildren.

A seventieth birthday portrait, a photograph by Cecil Beaton of the Queen Mother sitting outside Clarence House in 1970.

Anne knowing of her great interest in eventing. The party was held in Whitbread's famous Cellars near Ludgate Circus in London. One of those invited was the reserve rider, Officer Cadet Mark Phillips of Sandhurst Military Academy, who was duly introduced to Princess Anne. It was probably the first time they met but did not then spark off any particular interest, apart from conversation on eventing and horses.

On 6th November 1968, the day after the great liner *Queen Elizabeth* was withdrawn from service, the Queen Mother came to Southampton to say a fond farewell to the ship she had launched thirty years earlier. This was another break with the past. It was a bright clear day and she stepped aboard just before noon. After talking to members of the crew, the Captain, Commodore Geoffrey Marr, and the Chairman of Cunard escorted her to the Promenade Deck where she was introduced to the ship's officers. At lunch in the Verandah Grill she was presented with a set of glass goblets to commemorate the final voyage, a cruise to Las Palmas, and in a short speech she told them how keenly she had followed the ship's career. After lunch she visited the public rooms and the bridge. The great ship was sold to an American company but in 1972 was destroyed by fire.

The investiture of the Prince of Wales was the great event of 1969, second only to the Coronation in its splendour. The Queen Mother proudly watched the Queen investing Prince Charles as the twenty-first Prince at Caernarvon Castle. The Queen Mother and her grandson have a tremendous rapport for each other. 'He is more like a son than a grandson', she once said; the son that she never had.

In fact, there is a close bond of affection between the Royal grandmother and all her grandchildren. Two were born in Clarence House, Princess Anne and David, Viscount Linley. Prince Andrew, who gained his laurels as a helicopter pilot in the Falklands War, always appears especially affectionate to her as does his younger brother Prince Edward and his exact contemporary, Lady Sarah Armstrong-Jones. Now there is a rising generation of four great-grandchildren – Princess Anne's two, Peter and Zara Phillips, and the Prince of Wales's two sons, Prince William and Prince Harry.

The Queen Mother with Princess Margaret and Princess Beatrix of the Netherlands attends the wedding of her great-niece Lady Elizabeth Anson and Sir Geoffrey Shakerley.

For many years every September the Queen Mother gave a party at Birkhall for the younger members of the Royal Family and their friends. She hired a three-piece band from Aberdeen for this popular occasion.

On 28th May 1972 the Duke of Windsor died and his widow was invited by the Queen to stay at Buckingham Palace for the funeral at St. George's Chapel, Windsor. He was buried at Frogmore near Windsor. The Queen Mother ended all bitterness between them by trying to comfort her, 'I know. I have been through it all myself'. Dr. Jean Thin,

the Duchess of Windsor's French doctor, observed them closely and said that Queen Elizabeth was 'kindness itself'. Now these two widows are the only main characters of the Abdication drama still living and one of them, the Duchess of Windsor, is now incapacitated.

During that July the Queen Mother and Prince Charles attended the wedding at Barnwell Church in Northamptonshire, of Prince Richard, the younger of the Duke of Gloucester's two sons, to Miss Birgitte van Deurs. The Queen was in Scotland at the time. The wedding was not held in Denmark where the bride lived so that the bridegroom's father could be present at least at the reception. He had suffered several strokes and was now a complete invalid.

Only a month after the wedding tragedy befell the Gloucester family. Prince William, the Duke's elder son, aged thirty, handsome and charming, was killed in an air-race accident. Audrey Whiting recorded a glowing tribute the Prince paid to his aunt the Queen Mother. 'If I let myself down – say I get into a mess of some sort – my first thought would be that the Queen Mother would feel that I let her down. I have always felt like this even as a young child. It isn't that she ever said anything. It's a sort of indescribable sense of dedication she gave me.' He added, 'I can't tell you what the Queen Mother means to all of us. You only have to be loved by her – and to love her yourself – to know that, no matter what, you could never let her down.'

Only two years later the Duke of Gloucester died at Barnwell. He was the King's last surviving brother, and his passing meant the severing of one more link with the past. His body lay in state at Victoria Barracks, Windsor, as was fitting for a soldier Prince. In the procession through the town of Windsor, his personal charger, 'Bugle Boy' aged thirteen from the stables of the Scots Guards, immediately preceded the coffin.

The Queen and Prince Philip celebrated their Silver Wedding anniversary in November 1972. The day began with a thanksgiving service at Westminster Abbey. That evening the Prince of Wales and Princess Anne hosted a dinner party at Buckingham Palace where the English Chamber Orchestra played the Wedding March and the Bach Choir sang the anthems they had performed at their wedding. The Queen Mother was a leading member of their specially selected guests.

Princess Anne's engagement to Captain Mark Phillips was announced in May 1973, and their wedding took place on Prince Charles' birthday, 14th November, at Westminster Abbey. The Queen Mother wearing beige and gold sat with the Queen, the Prince of Wales and Prince Andrew in the Scottish State Coach in the procession to the Abbey. The tradition she established in 1923 of having a golden wedding ring from Welsh gold was followed for her granddaughter and later for her grandson the Prince of Wales. Afterwards she said that the bride and bridegroom had so many interests in common that they could almost have been computer-dated!

Painting by Michael Noakes to commemorate the Silver Wedding of the Queen and Prince Philip in 1972, when the Royal Family were received at the Guildhall by the Lord Mayor of London. The Queen Mother is talking to Princess Anne and the Prince of Wales.

Opposite:
The Queen Mother in the
Drawing Room at
Clarence House in a
formal gown of white
chiffon embroidered with
gold beads and wearing a
diamond tiara.
Photograph by Norman
Parkinson for her seventy-
fifth birthday.

The Queen Mother has been President of the Royal College of Music since her daughter relinquished the position when she succeeded as Queen. Previous to that she was Patron, as is now the Queen. In 1973 the Queen conferred upon her the Honorary Doctorate of Music, which she herself conferred upon her grandson, the Prince of Wales, eight years later. The Queen Mother and her grandson are both accomplished musicians – her instrument is the piano, his the cello.

In November 1974 the Queen Mother, as Chancellor of the University of London, conferred the Honorary degree of Doctor of Laws on the Prince of Wales. In his speech at the Senate House the Prince attacked pessimists. 'We are a great nation of self-depreciators. We are having a field day at the moment', he said. 'We must retain our sense of humour and ability to laugh at ourselves.'

The Queen Mother flew back to Canada that year to visit two of her Regiments, the Toronto Scottish and The Black Watch of Canada. She also presented the Gold Awards of the Duke of Edinburgh's Awards Scheme. In April 1975 she went to Iran for five days as a guest of the Shah who a few years afterwards was sent into exile. Much to her regret, she was unable to fly out in the Concorde at 2,179kph (1,354mph) and had to take the Royal Air Force Comet, travelling at only 805kph (500mph). She toured the Iran Bastan Museum to see their many archaeological treasures and then to the glorious ruins of Persepolis, one of the chief cities of ancient Persia, which was probably founded by Cyrus. She went on to Isfahan, 200 miles in circuit and is one of the most interesting cities in Iran. The Shah presented her with a magnificent carpet. On her return she had lunch at the Royal Air Force Base at Akrotiri in Cyprus. In the following year her hostess Farah, the Shahbanou of Iran, returned her visit to stay at Clarence House, and became quite a favourite. Her photograph is now at Clarence House.

In 1974 the Queen Mother deputized for her daughter, the Queen, then in Mexico, as one of the six Counsellors of State, before leaving in the Royal Yacht Britannia for a tour of the Channel Islands and the Isle of Wight. On their return a singular happening caught the attention of the press. As Her Majesty was stepping ashore from the royal barge on to the floating pontoon at Portsmouth, her handbag slipped out of her hand in the 15cm (6in) gap between the barge and the pontoon. Lieutenant Hugh Slade immediately flung himself on the ground face downwards and managed to get a finger into the strap of the bag, just as it was disappearing into the Solent. Queen Elizabeth complimented the Lieutenant for 'the finest salvage job ever carried out by the Royal Navy' and later sent him a personally written letter of thanks and a pair of cufflinks.

For the Queen Mother's seventy-fifth birthday on 4th August 1975, messages of congratulations poured in throughout the day. A large crowd sang 'Happy Birthday' outside Clarence House. Instead of the usual quiet family birthday party, the Queen and Prince Philip gave her a surprise dinner party of about eighty people at Buckingham Palace. The menu was Avocado Pears with Crab, Saddle of Lamb, Beans, Carrots and Potatoes, Chocolate Mousse and Dessert. Pipe Majors of the Queen and the Queen Mother piped their way around the tables.

Benjamin Britten, founder of the Aldeburgh Festival, had composed a special piece of music for her, a setting for seven of Robert Burns's poems. According to Peter Pears, they both went to Sandringham soon afterwards to present the album with the original score. He wrote, 'It was awfully touching. She is such a kind and loving person and wants to bring happiness.' Benjamin Britten was very ill at the time and died ten days afterwards. Later Peter Pears gave a public performance of the songs.

The Queen Mother spent four days of spring in 1976 visiting her beloved France. This time she went to see the Cathedrals and Castles of Burgundy. In September she went to the Sorbonne in Paris and during her visit had lunch with the French President, Monsieur Giscard d'Estaing and his wife, at the Elysée Palace. Sadly the marriage of Princess Margaret and Lord Snowdon had broken up. Their divorce was granted two years later. Although he has since remarried, Lord Snowdon's friendship with the Royal Family has continued and he still takes many of the official Royal photographs, including those of Prince Harry's christening at Christmas 1984.

There were three more holidays in France between 1977 and 1979. First Her Majesty stayed for three days with Baron Philippe de Rothschild at his Château Mouton in the Médoc. He is one of the principal wine-growers in the world, and incidentally grows and bottles Her Majesty's favourite wine. The label on the 1977 bottle bore her name in honour of her stay. Then she went to the

Dordogne to stay at the Château de Hautefort. On her third visit she had a week in Lorraine as the guest of Prince de Beauvau-Craon at the Château de Haroué.

1977 was the year of the Queen's Silver Jubilee. In the procession to St. Paul's Cathedral the Queen Mother sat with her two grandsons, Prince Andrew and Prince Edward, immediately before the Queen and Prince Philip in the golden State Coach, used for the first time since the Coronation. The Queen, speaking at the Guildhall, concluded, 'My Lord Mayor, when I was twenty-one I pledged *my life* to the service of our people and I asked for God's help to make that vow. Although that vow was made "in my salad days when I was green in judgement", I do not retract one word of it.' This is as good an answer as any to people who ask if the Queen is ever likely to abdicate!

On 15th August, the twenty-seventh birthday of Princess Anne, the Queen Mother welcomed twenty-four members of the Royal Family as her guests at the Castle of Mey for lunch. In the afternoon they played games on the beach and in the evening the party continued in the Royal Yacht *Britannia*. Then at 7.30 p.m. the Queen Mother returned to her castle and the Royal Yacht sailed away amid a blaze of flares.

Princess Anne gave birth on 15th November to the Queen Mother's first great-grandchild Peter Phillips, thus a Jubilee baby, to everyone's delight. 'It's marvellous', said his great grandmother. Peter was the first grandchild of a monarch to be born without any title for at least 474 years.

A historic office was granted to the Queen Mother in 1979, that of Lord Warden of the Cinque Ports and Constable of Dover Castle. Many famous names had filled this office, including the great Duke of Wellington, Sir Winston Churchill and her immediate predecessor, Sir Robert Menzies.

Opposite:
The world was shocked at the assassination in Ireland of Earl Mountbatten of Burma. The Queen Mother with all the members of the Royal Family attends his funeral in Westminster Abbey 12th September 1979.

Right:
The Queen Mother was installed as Lord Warden of the Cinque Ports in August 1979, and is here inspecting the Guard of Honour at Dover Castle.

Below:
The New Lord Warden of the Cinque Ports in the procession down the hill at Dover.

Her Majesty sailed on board the Royal Yacht *Britannia* with three of her grandchildren, Prince Edward, Lord Linley and Lady Sarah Armstrong-Jones, and they went in the Scottish State Coach in procession through Dover. After the Hallowing Service in the Church of St. Mary in Castro (St. Mary in the Castle) the procession went down the hill to the ancient Priory of St. Martin, now Dover College, where she was installed as the 160th Lord Warden at a special meeting of the Grand Court of Shepway, held in a marquee on the broad lawn. Not only was she the first Royal Lord Warden, but also the first lady to fill that office.

Queen Elizabeth made an amusing speech and in it alluded to her male predecessors. 'Despite this revolutionary change, customs remain constant.' She has the right to the 'fishes royal' found in the confines of the Cinque Ports, to whales, porpoises and sturgeon. There is, however, a troublesome rider, the Lord Warden must pay for the burial of stranded whales!

After being given lunch at the Town Hall, the Maison Dieu, her first function as Lord Warden, the Queen Mother invited the Barons and Mayors of the Cinque Ports and other distinguished guests on board the Royal Yacht *Britannia*, berthed in Dover Harbour. Later that evening came a spectacular display by the Red Arrows, diving and

weaving over Dover Harbour. Then a firework display and just before midnight *Britannia* sailed away.

In August 1979 came the sudden shock of Lord Mountbatten's brutal assassination at Classiebawn, Ireland, when his boat was blown up by Irish terrorists. Also killed were the Dowager Lady Brabourne and his grandson Nicholas and another boy. The Queen came over from Balmoral to break the news to her mother at Birkhall. Lord Mountbatten was a second cousin of King George VI and an uncle of Prince Philip. No one felt the blow more than the Prince of Wales, who said 'I miss him so dreadfully'. The Queen Mother, and all the Royal Family, attended his funeral service at Westminster Abbey.

That September the Queen Mother went on a farewell visit to the Aircraft Carrier, H.M.S. *Ark Royal*, the largest ship in the Royal Navy, which was taken out of service three months later. She had launched the ship in 1950, and had always received a telegram of best wishes on her birthday. The ship's name is one of the oldest in the history of the Royal Navy. The original one was known as *Ark Raleigh* and was built by the Elizabethan courtier Sir Walter Raleigh and sold by him to Queen Elizabeth I, who renamed it *Ark Royal*. The immediate predecessor of this last *Ark Royal* was sunk in the Second World War. The Queen Mother had visited the ship in 1966, landing by helicopter on the flight deck. Seven years later Leeds conferred the Freedom of the City on *Ark Royal*. It was during this ceremony that the Queen Mother was seen giving a cough sweet to a sailor who had lost his voice. This farewell to *Ark Royal* must have been a memorable occasion.

The Queen Mother visited the aircraft carrier H.M.S. Ark Royal *at Devonport in July 1958.*

Eighty Years On

1980 was the year of the Queen Mother, in which she celebrated her eightieth birthday. Festivities started in midsummer. On 18th June, in the middle of Ascot Week, the Queen gave her a glittering ball at Windsor Castle jointly with two contemporaries who were also born in 1900. These were her sister-in-law Princess Alice, Duchess of Gloucester, whose actual birthday fell on the following Christmas Day and the Duke of Beaufort in April, who died three years later.

Six hundred guests danced to the strains of Joe Loss, the Queen Mother's favourite band leader. Among the Ascot house party was the tall and vivacious Queen Margrethe of Denmark, just installed as a Lady of the Garter, with her husband Prince Henrik, and the Grand Duke and Duchess of Luxembourg.

In early July an extra 1,000 guests were invited to the garden party at the Palace of Holyroodhouse, including many of the Queen Mother's old friends to whom she chatted for an hour and a half. On the following day a musical tribute was paid to her in Holyrood Park by 300 pipes, drums and regimental bands of six Scottish regiments, and in the evening a reception at Holyroodhouse was held. The Queen Mother, looking much younger than her years, took part in Scottish reels, wearing her tartan sash over a sparkling evening dress.

The main event was a special Birthday Thanksgiving Service held at St. Paul's Cathedral on 15th July. It was the Queen's wish to remain in the background as much as possible and she accorded her mother two special privileges on that day by yielding precedence to her. The first was for the Queen Mother to have the Sovereign's Escort of Household Cavalry to and from St. Paul's, and the second, for her to be the last to arrive there and the first to leave.

The Queen Mother inspects the Chelsea Pensioners at the Royal Hospital, Chelsea, in June 1980.

A study by Norman Parkinson of Her Majesty on her eightieth birthday.

The Queen Mother's triumphal drive to St. Paul's Cathedral for her Eightieth Birthday Thanksgiving Service, escorted by the Prince of Wales.

Dressed in violet blue, the Queen Mother left Clarence House in the 1902 State Landau with her grandson the Prince of Wales wearing naval uniform, on her triumphal progress to St. Paul's, for so it proved to be. When they reached the Cathedral she waved to the cheering multitudes from the steps where she was received by the Lord Mayor of London and then joined by the Queen and other members of the Royal Family. A fanfare of trumpets heralded her procession up the nave. The great Service of Thanksgiving was ecumenical as she had wished. The Dean of St. Paul's was assisted by the Moderator of the Church of Scotland who read the lesson and Cardinal Hume who said

two prayers. Dr. Runcie, the new Archbishop of Canterbury, gave the address, and when he referred to her and the late King in the East End of London during the blitz it was noticed that she had tears in her eyes. Archbishop Runcie described the service as 'the most beautiful I've taken'.

When the Service was over the Queen Mother left amid fervent cheering all along the route, this time escorted by Prince Philip on the return journey to Buckingham Palace.

After this splendid ceremony, there came on the following day a small one at the Rose Walk in St. James's Park, nearly opposite Clarence House. Mr. Edward Wagg, President of the National Gardens Association,

In July 1980 a reception at the Palace of Holyroodhouse, Edinburgh, formed part of the Queen Mother's eightieth birthday celebrations. She appears here with the Queen, Prince Philip, the Prince of Wales and Princess Margaret.

presented to Her Majesty seven young gardeners and two seniors who had been responsible for laying out the Rose Garden under his auspices, paid for by public subscription. She then planted a rose bush to commemorate her eightieth birthday. This was not a dainty turn of the earth but a hearty dig with a silver spade appropriate for the doyenne of royal gardeners.

The Queen gave her mother a garden party at Buckingham Palace on 17th July to which she invited representatives of the 300 or so organizations of which she is Patron or President, some going back to when she was Duchess of York.

Later that month the Royal Tournament had a double celebration. It was their centenary year and they gave the Queen Mother a special tribute in which all her Regiments, including those of the Commonwealth, took part. To each team she applauded enthusiastically. The pipe tune 'The Castle of Mey', by Lieutenant-Colonel Duncan Beat, was spe-cially commissioned for the occasion and played by the Queen Mother's personal piper from The London Scottish.

The actual birthday celebrations started at midnight with the arrival of eighty red roses from the members of the Royal Philharmonic Orchestra, of which she is Patron. Among similar tributes, representatives of the late Sir Norman Hartnell, her couturier, who used to send her roses to match her years, sent her eighty in his memory.

A large crowd gathered outside Clarence House from 7.00 a.m., which soon amounted to about 3,000. Time after time they sang 'Happy Birthday' and 'For She's a Jolly Good Fellow'. Many floated gaily coloured balloons bearing the messages 'Happy Birthday Queen Mum' and 'We Love you Queen Mum'. They were rewarded just after 11.00 a.m. when, wearing a blue dress and hat, she made the first of several balcony appearances. She waved to the crowd and repeatedly said 'Thank you very much.' The band of the

Opposite:
Inside St. Paul's Cathedral for the Queen Mother's Birthday Service in 1981, with the Queen and Prince Philip.

Below:
A visit to the 1983 Royal Tournament at Earls Court. The Queen Mother meets a member of the R.A.F. Parachute Regiment who form the guard of honour.

Welsh Guards joined in the celebrations by playing 'Happy Birthday' as they marched down Stable Yard past Clarence House.

Inside was a sea of flowers. For some days an enormous mail had poured into Clarence House, followed by eight more sackfuls on her birthday morning. The front doorbell rang continuously as footmen and staff collected letters, presents and flowers by armfuls. Then the Queen Mother made her appearance through the double gates to loud cheering. Standing a few paces behind her were the Queen, Prince Edward and Princess Margaret with her son and daughter. Then many children came forward to present their bunches of flowers and have a few words with the delighted Queen Mother. So many flowers were there that the Queen and Princess Margaret helped to take them inside.

At noon ten Jet Provost trainer planes from the R.A.F. Central Flying School, of which the Queen Mother is Commandant-in-Chief, flew over central London in an 'E' formation.

Simultaneously the King's Troop, Royal Horse Artillery, fired their salute of forty-one guns from Hyde Park. Seventy-one horses took part, with officers and soldiers in their colourful ceremonial full dress. The scene as they galloped away was reminiscent of the Napoleonic wars. An hour later the Honourable Artillery Company, oldest regiment in the British Army, fired their royal salute from the Tower of London, in this case of sixty-two guns.

Celebrations extended to the country. St. Paul's Walden and Whitwell put on a lakeside concert, an open day at her old home the Bury, a flower festival and a photographic exhibition in All Saints Church. Ham in Surrey had an open day at Forbes House, her grandmother's home where she often stayed as a child and is now an old people's centre. Beacons were lit from bonfires that straddled the coast of Kent and Sussex as was done at the Coronation and Jubilee, in this case to honour the Queen Mother's appointment as Lord Warden of the Cinque Ports.

B.B.C. Scotland presented a special programme, narrated by Tom Fleming, and a fine series of postage stamps were issued by the Post Office in England and by several countries in the Commonwealth, their Associated States and Dependencies. Nune, in the South Pacific, chose an impressive one of her coat of arms, while one of Lesotho in Southern Africa, bears an inset of the stamp issued in 1947 for the visit of King George VI

and Queen Elizabeth to Basutoland, its former name. Others include Bangladesh, Bahamas, Gibraltar and Antigua.

On her birthday evening the Queen Mother, with the Queen and her family, attended a gala performance at Covent Garden of Sir Frederick Ashton's ballet 'Rhapsody'. Princess Margaret had urged him to choreograph a ballet for her mother. Her

Above:
Outside Clarence House on the Queen Mother's eightieth birthday, when many people carried balloons with the message 'We love you, Queen Mum'.

Left:
The Royal Family greet Queen Elizabeth on her eightieth birthday. Two of her grandchildren were missing, Prince Andrew and Princess Anne.

Right:
Warrant Officer Bob
Smith presents Queen
Elizabeth with the cake
he baked for her eightieth
birthday.

Below:
Sculptor Oscar Nemon
with his portrait bust of
Queen Elizabeth in
October 1980.

Majesty told her friend Freddie Ashton it was the nicest birthday present she had ever received. After the National Anthem and 'Happy Birthday', sung with great feeling, silver rain poured from the ceiling. To conclude the evening, the entire company assembled on the stage to share her massive birthday cake with pink and white icing, after she blew out the single candle.

Three special birthday photographs by Norman Parkinson were released and added to the Exhibition of her Portraits and Pictures at the National Portrait Gallery. Two showed Her Majesty with her daughters: in the first, dressed in blue capes, which Mr. Parkinson pointed out will go down in history as being timeless, for there is no fashion to date it. 'It was their idea,' he said. The second shows them in day dress, holding hands in the gardens at Windsor, and the third of the

The Queen Mother and
Sir Frederick Ashton
celebrate her eightieth
birthday at Covent
Garden by sharing a piece
of birthday cake.

Queen Mother looking out of a window at Clarence House. Another photographic exhibition and display of her wedding dress was held in the Norman Undercroft of Westminster Abbey.

On the following morning Her Majesty travelled to the solitude of her little Castle of Mey, no doubt for a well-earned rest.

The press had been marrying off Prince Charles ever since he was a small boy, but during the last few years a campaign by certain unscrupulous photographers and publications had reached an unbearable extent. Any girl who was spotted out with him became his prospective bride and, if possible, photographs were taken. First it was Davina Sheffield, then the Duke of Wellington's daughter Lady Jane Wellesley, and many others.... In September 1980 a reporter discovered that a young visitor to Balmoral was the daughter of Earl Spencer, Lady Diana Spencer, who lived with three flatmates at Colherne Court, Old Brompton Road in South Kensington and taught in a kindergarten. The press continually hounded her, an awful ordeal for a nineteen-year-old. During that autumn the Prince of Wales went on a long-awaited tour of India leaving Lady Diana to cope with the press, which she did admirably under the circumstances, until his return in December.

On Tuesday 24th February 1981 the Queen announced the Prince's engagement to Lady Diana Spencer. No one could have been more pleased than the Queen Mother. It has been said that the Prince unofficially told her before the Queen. It transpired that the two had stayed a week at Birkhall as the Queen Mother's guests before the Prince went out to India and again for a weekend on his return home. On the evening of their engagement they dined in celebration with the Queen Mother and Lady Diana's grandmother, Ruth Lady Fermoy, her lady-in-waiting and a close friend. Lady Diana immediately moved out of her flat to Clarence House, where for the next few days she was the Queen Mother's guest and was given a few lessons in royal protocol. Later a suite of rooms was prepared for her at Buckingham Palace where she remained until she returned to Clarence House the night before the wedding.

The Queen Mother and the Princess of Wales share much the same family background. Both are the daughters of earls, and they bear to each other a not very distant relationship of fifth cousins three times removed through their descent from the 3rd Duke of Devonshire. To balance Queen Elizabeth's Virginian ancestors, the Spencers also had kinship to George Washington. In addition the Princess has some exotic Ameri-

can cousins through Frances Work, mother of her grandfather Lord Fermoy. These include Humphrey Bogart, Lee Remick, Harriet Beecher Stowe, Louisa M. Alcott, Orson Welles and John Pierpoint Morgan. She is also a descendant of two Stuart Kings, Charles I and Charles II, missing from the Queen's pedigree, though admittedly through the Merry Monarch's mistresses.

Lady Diana Spencer was born and brought up at Park House, Sandringham, a near neighbour in Norfolk of the Royal Family.

Her grandfather, Lord Fermoy, had leased the house from King George V and then from King George VI. Just before Lord Fermoy died in 1955, his eighteen-year-old daughter Frances married Lord Althorp, later the 8th Earl Spencer, a marriage which unfortunately broke up. They have three daughters and one son, of whom the Princess of Wales is the youngest daughter. It is ironic that she alone of her brother and sisters does not have a royal godparent. Her mother is now the Hon. Mrs. Peter Shand Kydd.

Left:
The Queen Mother at eighty with her favourite corgi in the garden of Royal Lodge, Windsor.

Below:
The Queen and the Queen Mother talking to Alhaji Shehu Shagari, President of Nigeria at a banquet given in his honour in March 1981.

Soon after Lady Fermoy was widowed she became a lady-in-waiting to the Queen Mother. Her musical training led to her organizing and sometimes playing in lunchtime concerts, and in 1951 she launched the King's Lynn Festival, which the Queen Mother attends annually as Patron. Lady Fermoy is a fellow Scot, daughter of Colonel William Smith Gill of Dalhebity near Bieldside in Aberdeenshire. David Williamson the genealogist tells me that he compiled a chart for her that shows her descent from the

Regent Earl of Moray, Mary Queen of Scots' half-brother.

The Princess of Wales is related to several others who have served the Queen Mother. Of these her father's mother, Countess Spencer, acted as lady-in-waiting until her death in 1972, and her sister Lady Katharine Seymour long held this appointment before retiring in 1960. Diana's great-aunt by marriage, the Dowager Duchess of Abercorn, is the Queen Mother's Mistress of the Robes, and thus technically 'in charge' of the ladies-in-waiting. To complete these relationships, two sisters of her grandfather Earl Spencer were also ladies-in-waiting: Lady Annaly when the Queen Mother was Duchess of York, and Lady Delia Peel from 1939 to 1950. As *The Times* pointed out, the Queen Mother had as many Spencers round her at the Royal wedding as had the bride.

Her Majesty ensured that the Princess made as smooth a transition to the senior ranks of the Royal Family as did she herself all those years ago. To cross the great divide between the aristocracy and the Royal Family may have appeared daunting at first, even though her grandmother Lady Fermoy is steeped in court routine. No doubt the Queen Mother still continues to help the Prince and Princess of Wales when the occasion arises.

By coincidence, just as the Queen Mother had her Alla and King George VI his Lalla, the Princess of Wales had her Ally, as she called Miss Gertrude Allen. She was an elderly white-haired governess from the neighbouring village of Dersingham who came to Park House at Sandringham when the children were young, having once been their mother's governess. Sadly, Ally died a few weeks before the wedding.

In the interval between the announcement of the engagement and the wedding, the Queen Mother continued to be busily engaged. In May 1981 she received the Freedom of the Borough of Windsor and Maidenhead at a ceremony in the Home Park, and in the same month she launched the new carrier H.M.S. *Ark Royal* on Tyneside, a continuity of that historic name, having launched this ship's predecessor.

Princess Anne's daughter Zara was born on 15th May, the second of the Queen Mother's great-grandchildren. Princess Anne's magnificent work as President of The Save the Children Fund, which takes her to remote parts of the world, sometimes in danger and frequently in great discomfort, is dear to her grandmother's heart.

On 2nd July, despite an injury to her leg when she stumbled at the Garter Service, the Queen Mother went for a week's visit to Canada, flying to Toronto. Here she visited her regiments, the Toronto Scottish, the Canadian Forces Medical Services and an element of The Black Watch who came over from Montreal. They combined to give a garden party in her honour. She also visited Niagara, then celebrating its bicentenary, and attended the Queen's Plate at the Woodbine Race Track, Toronto. At the end of her tour the Queen Mother met Princess Margaret, accompanied for the first time by her seventeen-year-old daughter Lady Sarah: they had flown out in connection with the fiftieth anniversary celebrations of the Royal Ballet.

As there have been many books written on the wedding of Prince Charles and Lady Diana Spencer, it will be enough to say here that the 26th July 1981 was a superb day when London was *en fête* and everyone took the bride to their hearts. The usual quiet of Clarence House was broken early in the morning, when the bride rose and began to prepare for the great event with her hairdressers, couturiers and assistance from her mother and sisters. The bridesmaids, too, of whom Lady Sarah Armstrong-Jones was the chief, also prepared for the great event ahead.

At precisely 10.22 a.m. the Queen Mother, dressed in eau-de-nil, left in the second carriage in the Queen's procession from Buckingham Palace with Prince Edward, aged seventeen. It was his first major royal occasion, for he and Prince Andrew were the Prince of Wales' two supporters, as was traditional instead of a best man.

Then at 10.37 a.m. the radiant bride left Clarence House with her father Lord Spencer in the glass coach with an escort of mounted police, just as in 1923 had Lady Elizabeth Bowes-Lyon on her marriage to the Duke of York. St. Paul's had not seen a royal wedding since 1501 when Arthur Prince of Wales married Catherine of Aragon, who later wed his brother Henry VIII.

After the departure of the Prince and Princess of Wales on their honeymoon, first to Broadlands, home of the late Lord Mountbatten of Burma, and then aboard the Royal Yacht *Britannia* for a cruise in the Mediterranean, the Queen with the Queen Mother and other members of the Royal Family went for a private party at Claridge's. This had been arranged by the Queen Mother's great-niece, Lady Elizabeth Shakerley, sister of the celebrated photographer Lord Lichfield.

Above:
At the christening at Windsor of Zara Phillips in August 1981, Princess Anne holds her baby daughter and sits between the Queen, Peter and the Queen Mother.

Right:
The Queen Mother waves to the workers on the site of Lloyd's new building in Leadenhall Street in London, which she inaugurated in November 1981.

After the excitement of 1981, the next year was to have some dramatic happenings, but first there was the Queen Mother's carefully planned tour in April to that unhappy province of Ulster, during which she came to see one of her regiments, 1st The Queen's Dragoon Guards, at Lisanelly Barracks in Omagh, Co. Tyrone. This was her first time in Ulster since 1969. So tight were the security arrangments that news of her five-hour stay was only released after she had returned home.

Without any provocation, on 2nd April 1982 Argentina invaded and occupied the Falkland Islands. Britain immediately sent a Task Force which sailed via Ascension Island across the South Atlantic, a most difficult and hazardous manoeuvre. The country was overwhelmingly behind this operation and the sudden wave of patriotism had not been seen since the Second World War.

Prince Andrew, a Fleet Air Arm helicopter pilot attached to H.M.S. *Invincible*, played a significant part in this short and sharp campaign. The Cunard liner *Queen Elizabeth II* was converted from a luxury liner to trans-

port men of the 5th Infantry Brigade to the Falklands.

After the war was fought and won, QE2 returned to Britain with the survivors from Her Majesty's Ships *Ardent*, *Antelope* and *Coventry*, and received a heroes' welcome on 11th June when she docked at Southampton. The Queen Mother was aboard *Britannia* for duties on the South Coast, she diverted the Royal Yacht to rendezvous in the West Solent with the great liner. For a few minutes the two ships came close enough for her to wave her greeting of thanks and she sent a message saying 'I am proud of you all'. Prince Andrew and his colleagues continued to patrol the exclusion zone around the Falklands and did not arrive back at Portsmouth until 17th September. Then he jumped for joy and threw his hat in the air when he was welcomed home by his parents and Princess Anne.

On 7th June President and Mrs. Ronald Reagan arrived on a State Visit and stayed at Windsor Castle, making history as the first President of the United States to stay in a royal residence in Britain. At a dinner party

given to them that evening the Queen Mother was present.

The next morning the Queen went on her much publicized ride with the President, while Prince Philip escorted Mrs. Reagan in his four-in-hand carriage. The Queen Mother left that morning by helicopter bound for Margate, but soon after taking off had to make a forced landing on Smith's Lawn, Windsor. The pilot said that she was 'totally unshaken' by the episode. This did not apply to the damaged surface of Smith's Lawn, the Guards' Polo Club ground. Her Majesty and to a lesser extent, Princess Anne, are the only Royal ladies addicted to the red 'chopper'. The Queen and Princess Alexandra both detest the noise of this form of transport.

As a result of this delay, the morning visits to Margate and Ramsgate had to be cancelled, but Her Majesty was able to fulfil her afternoon engagements in Canterbury and Faversham. She then visited the 'ancient towns' of Rye and Winchelsea, which had been added to the original Cinque Ports, and their 'limbs' of Tenterden, Lydd, Folkestone and Deal.

On the steps of St. Paul's Cathedral after attending the Falkland Islands' Service in 1982, the Queen Mother leaves with the Prince and Princess of Wales, Princess Anne and Captain Mark Phillips.

Prince Andrew was still serving in the Falklands when that very important baby Prince William, second in line to the throne, was born to the Princess of Wales on 21st June 1982 at St. Mary's Hospital, Paddington. He was also away for the christening, which took place in the Music Room at Buckingham Palace on the Queen Mother's eighty-second birthday on 4th August. Though the little Prince was quiet at the christening and signing of the register, tears began to flow when they all assembled in the Blue Drawing Room for a photograph session. Only his mother's finger would quieten him. The Queen Mother who proudly held her great-grandson observed 'he has a good pair of lungs'. Afterwards she was the principal guest at luncheon for both celebrations.

During dinner at Royal Lodge on 21st November, a fishbone became lodged in the Queen Mother's throat. A guest, Hugh Cavendish, said that all he could do was to stop her from being so polite. 'I had to persuade her to stop trying to make conversation and gave her a slap on the back.'

Princess Margaret immediately escorted her by car speeding along the M4 Motorway to King Edward VII Hospital in London, where an operation to remove the fishbone was successfully undertaken that night. This was a serious matter for a lady of her age, and she was disappointed at having to miss a reception at Buckingham Palace for the Diplomatic Corps and a Gala performance at Covent Garden. Eight days after the operation she fulfilled her appointment at the Court of Patrons at the Royal College of Obstetricians and Gynaecologists. Needless to say, press photographers and cameras were out in force.

The Queen Mother went by helicopter on 1st December to Southampton to unveil a plaque in the Queen's Room of R.M.S. *Queen Elizabeth II* to commemorate the ship's part in the Falklands campaign. She talked to the men of the 5th Infantry Brigade, and the paratroops who had fought so bravely in the Falklands.

When the Prince and Princess of Wales left in March 1983 for their tour of Australia

A family occasion, the christening of Prince William was held at Buckingham Palace on the Queen Mother's birthday 1982. The Princess of Wales holds the baby, with the Queen and Queen Mother sitting by her, while Prince Charles stands behind.

The Queen Mother welcoming Prince Andrew and Prince Edward at Thurso on a visit to her Castle of Mey.

Queen Beatrix of the Netherlands gives a State Banquet at Hampton Court Palace in November 1982. The Queen, the Queen Mother and others of the Royal Family are greeted on arrival.

and New Zealand taking their nine-month-old son Prince William with them, the Queen Mother must have thought back to the time when she had to leave her own young daughter Princess Elizabeth in 1927 during their nine-months tour of the same countries.

In April the Queen Mother visited Brixton in South London, including Railton Road which, two years previously had been the centre of some ugly race riots and virtually a 'no go' area. During Her Majesty's trip to open a new purpose-built day centre, she talked to the inhabitants of Brixton of all ages, who gave her a warm welcome. She was particularly glad to talk to so many young children.

In June the Queen Mother flew to Northern Ireland for the celebrations of the seventy-fifth anniversary of the Territorial Army in Ulster, taking the salute at Ballymena, Co. Antrim. She stayed at Hillsborough Castle as the guest of the Secretary of State, James Prior and his wife Jane. Queen Elizabeth often visited Hillsborough where her sister Rose and her husband Lord Granville lived for seven

years when he was Governor of Northern Ireland. She was pleased to find that Mr. Harpur, butler in the Granvilles' time, still held that post.

Queen Elizabeth flew to Oslo for a weekend in July to attend King Olav's eightieth birthday celebrations. 'That little English lady with the King who keeps smiling' was on everybody's lips but she was careful not to wave back, allowing King Olav to receive all the thunder. When the great birthday banquet in Akershus Castle ended after midnight, the Queen Mother appeared as fresh as ever. A posy of flowers was presented to her on leaving. She smiled graciously and handed them to King Olav. 'These are for you', she laughed.

King Olav was born at Appleton House on the Sandringham estate which King Edward VII had given to his daughter Queen Maud of Norway, Olav's mother. Appropriately enough, the Queen Mother's birthday gift to him was a little porcelain box engraved with 'Appleton'. King Olav usually comes to London to do his Christmas shopping, and often attends the Festival of Remembrance at the Royal Albert Hall and Remembrance Sunday at the Cenotaph as he did that year. The Queen was then attending the Common-wealth Conference at New Delhi, when the Prince of Wales laid her wreath.

When the Queen Mother unveiled the tablet to the memory of Sir Nöel Coward in Westminster Abbey on 28th March 1984, some of his entrancing songs were played during the service which must have brought the congregation great feelings of nostalgia for 'the Master'. He was the Queen Mother's guest at Clarence House for luncheon on his seventieth birthday in 1969, when the Queen asked him if he would accept Sir Harold Wilson's recommendation for a knighthood. On the tablet were the words 'A Talent to Amuse' taken from his 1929 musical play 'Bitter Sweet'. Sir Nöel died in his beloved Jamaica in March 1973.

The Queen Mother left Portsmouth on board the Royal Yacht *Britannia* on 29th May for a tour of the Channel Islands. She began by visiting Guernsey on the 30th. After attending a service in the Town Church and fulfilling a large number of engagements she went to a lunch party at Government House. Then in the afternoon she toured the island by car through roads lined with waving and cheering people and inspected the Scouts and Guides. After a full schedule she gave a small dinner party on board *Britannia*, which was followed by a firework display.

From Guernsey she left by helicopter on 31st May for the little island of Alderney where she opened the Museum Extension and unveiled a plaque commemorating the visit. A 'Vin d'Honneur' was held in the Island Hall. A helicopter took her on to Sark, where she went to lunch with the Seigneur, Michael Beaumont, by horse-drawn carriage, for no motor cars are allowed in Sark. In the afternoon she visited an exhibition of children's work in the school hall and afterwards attended a reception for eighty people.

On the next day, 1st June, she landed from *Britannia* by barge at 10.15. After a heavy programme of engagements including visiting the Royal National Lifeboat Institution, Jersey Station, then celebrating its centenary, and opening the Maufant Youth Centre, where she showed her prowess at pool by potting a red to everyone's delight, and visiting Grainville School, she lunched at Government House. In the afternoon Her Majesty toured the island, glorious in the flowers that make Jersey justly famous. The rousing welcome for this magical lady who seemed ageless was on everyone's lips.

In the evening she gave a large dinner party on board *Britannia* for fifty-four people,

The Queen Mother aboard H.M. Royal Yacht Britannia *at Portsmouth 1982.*

In 1978 the Queen Mother inspects the Overlord Embroidery made over a period of seven years by the Royal School of Needlework, of which she is Patron. This depicts the story of the Second World War down to D-Day.

which was followed by a firework display, lighting up Elizabeth Castle.

Her Majesty had visited the Channel Islands twice since she and the King came in June 1945 immediately after the Channel Islands had been liberated from the Germans, namely in 1972 and 1975, but no welcome exceeded that given in 1984.

After these three days of engagements from 10.00 a.m. until midnight, when Her Majesty never appeared to have been the slightest bit tired, she continued her heavy programme by visiting Portsmouth. After lunch aboard *Britannia* on 2nd June she opened a block of flats for elderly ex-service people and their dependants at St. George's Court, Southsea. The Queen Mother is co-Patron of the Church of England Soldiers', Sailors' and Airmen's Club, and this is one of their housing schemes. Later she held a reception on board *Britannia* for D-Day veterans.

On 3rd June the Queen Mother attended the service in Portsmouth Cathedral to mark the fortieth anniversary of D-Day on 6th June 1944 and afterwards met officials and committee members of the D-Day and Normandy Fellowship, some of whom she had met on board the previous evening.

On the following day Queen Elizabeth unveiled the Overlord Panels Permanent Exhibition at the new D-Day Museum at Portsmouth.

The main attraction is the great 83m (272ft) long Embroidery covering the history of the war down to the D-Day landings of 'Operation Overlord'. This is 12.50m (41ft) longer than the Bayeux Tapestry, of which it is a modern-day counterpart, and is the largest work of its kind in the world. Lord Dulverton commissioned the Embroidery from the Royal School of Needlework, one of the Queen Mother's favourite patronages, in which she succeeded Queen Mary in 1953. This fine work took over seven years to complete and the School are justly proud of it.

On the following day the Queen Mother was back in London, where she unveiled one of London's 'blue plaques' that mark the houses of the famous. This one is at 4 Carlton Gardens, the London Headquarters in the war of General Charles de Gaulle when he was leader of the Free French. The Queen Mother, unlike many politicians, always got on well with this outstanding French leader.

Seldom in Her Majesty's life had she undertaken a more spectacular trip than her four-day visit to the City of Venice at the end of October 1984. She flew to Ancona on the Adriatic coast and from there sailed to Venice in the Royal Yacht *Britannia*, anchoring in the Grand Canal off St. Mark's Square.

The main purpose of her visit was to give royal blessing to the British Venice in Peril

Fund which, with other organizations, had spent nearly £500,000 ($555,000) in restoring buildings, paintings and monuments after the disastrous floods in 1966. She officially opened the little Oratorio dei Crociferi one of the masterpieces that had been recently restored. The President of the Fund, Sir Ashley Clarke, a former Ambassador to Italy, and John Julius Norwich (Viscount Norwich), the Chairman, were her principal guides.

Harassed carabinieri were sometimes hard pressed to make a path for the Queen Mother through the milling throng, but she was delighted to be there. On her arrival she said 'Doesn't the mist make Venice look romantic?' She saw St. Mark's Basilica and its celebrated mosaics, the Doge's Palace with the newly restored carving of the Porta della Carta and one of Venice's oldest churches, St. Nicolo dei Mendicoli, which was badly ruined with cracked doors and crumbling roof until restored in 1977. Also, the great Church of St. Giovanni and Paolo, where she was shown the magnificent fifteenth-century glass window depicting St. George and the Dragon.

Outside the church an Italian mama who had been waiting for some time could do nothing to quieten her howling three-months-old baby son. The Queen Mother walked over and gave the baby one of her freesias when he immediately stopped crying. She beamed with happiness at her success and after a walkabout in St. Mark's Square, she stopped for tea at the famous Florian's Café beneath the arcade. Her chief delight was her brief trip in a gondola, despite the mixed feelings of some of the organizers.

Her Majesty described her ten minute, 804m (880yd) excursion as 'magnifico, magnifico'. Oresto Dallacorte, one of Venice's leading gondoliers, took her and Admiral Paul Greening, Flag Officer Royal Yachts, in the newly painted black and gold gondola. She did not mind at all when the gondolier, for a joke, handed her a cornetto ice cream but this was quickly whisked away and replaced by a bunch of flowers. Afterwards

On Her Majesty's eighty-fourth birthday she appears outside Clarence House with three of her grandchildren, the Prince of Wales, Lady Sarah Armstrong-Jones and Viscount Linley.

Opposite:
A never-to-be-forgotten
occasion, a trip in a
gondola with Admiral
Paul Greening, Flag
Officer Royal Yachts.

Below:
The Queen Mother tours
Venice on her visit to
commemorate the
restoration carried out by
the Venice in Peril Fund,
October 1984.

she said 'It would have been such a shame to have come here without being able to take a spin in a gondola.'

Lady Clarke commented that 'the Queen Mother is in sparkling form. She adored all that chaos on the first day . . . She said she hadn't had so much fun for a long time.' Every minute possible she spent in sight-seeing and, despite her age, never appeared to tire, though some of her dinner parties in *Britannia* lasted until well after midnight. 'She can't wait to go back' a member of her Household said. A lifelong ambition to visit beautiful Venice was fulfilled.

Prince Henry, known to the Royal Family as Harry, younger son of the Prince and Princess of Wales, was born on 15th September and christened on 21st December 1984 at St. George's Chapel, the first day of their Christmas holiday at Windsor Castle. The last royal baby to be baptized there was Prince Harry's ancestor, the future King Edward VII, in 1842.

Harry was extremely well behaved and quiet, unlike his elder brother Prince William. The Queen Mother, who was filmed while holding him observed 'I really believe he is going to smile'. This delightful film was released on Christmas Day and incorporated into the Queen's Christmas message on television.

I have touched upon only a few of the Queen Mother's activities. Her main work concerns the regiments and units of which

she is Colonel-in-Chief or equivalent, and the 300 or so organizations of which she is Patron or President. She makes regular visits to them and watches their progress.

Her Majesty was the guest of honour at a tribute in the Albert Hall in January 1985 to twelve historic regiments, among them 1st The Queen's Dragoon Guards, The Queen's Own Hussars, The Royal Anglian Regiment, The King's Regiment and The Light Infantry, who celebrated their 300th birthday and

who enacted their history to the present day. The Light Infantry embodies The King's Own Yorkshire Light Infantry, to which she was appointed in 1927 when Duchess of York and which is her earliest Regiment as Colonel-in-Chief. Her regiments and units are listed on page 188.

Some of the Queen Mother's patronages are important national societies while others are small organizations. For instance she is Patron of the Royal Hospital and Home for

Overleaf:
At the christening in December 1984 of Prince Harry at Windsor Castle, the baby is held by his mother the Princess of Wales, beside the Queen and the Queen Mother, with the Prince of Wales perched behind his wife.

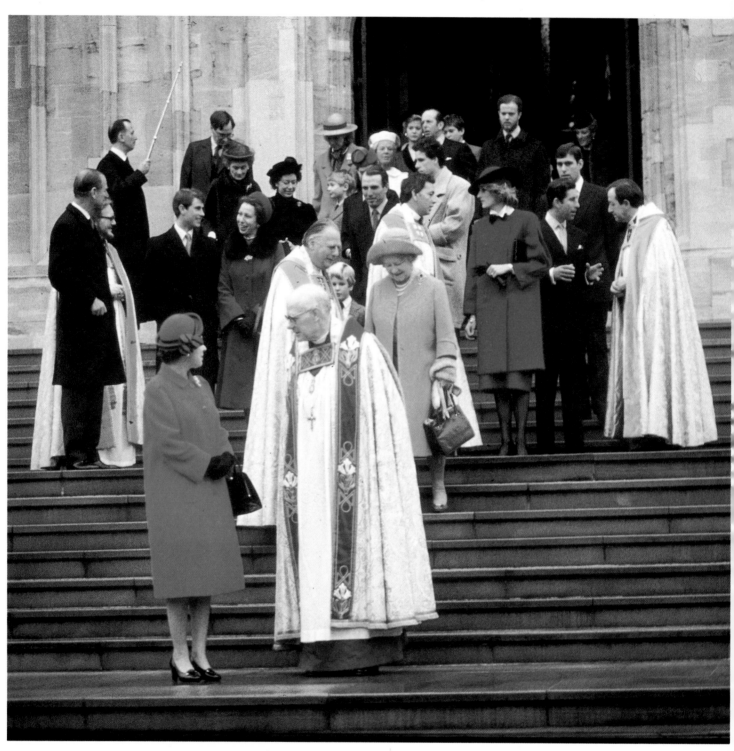

Above:
Leaving the 1984
Christmas Service at St.
George's Chapel,
Windsor.

Opposite:
The Queen Mother in
January 1985 at the
Albert Hall for the 300th
celebrations of twelve
historic regiments.

Incurables, Putney and the Young Women's Christian Association and President of the National Trust and the Women's Institute at Sandringham, in which she succeeded Queen Mary. Her wide interests accordingly are spread in many directions.

Of her many patronages, the earliest in origin is St. Katharine's Foundation now in Butcher Row in East London. This was founded by Matilda of Boulogne, wife of King Stephen, as the Royal Hospital of St. Katharine in East Smithfield, London. Ever since the Hospital was re-founded in 1273 by Queen Eleanor, Henry III's widow, Queens of England have been patrons for life. The

foundation moved to Regents Park in 1825 to make way for St. Katharine's Dock but in 1948 returned to East London. Once every two years the Queen Mother attends evensong and talks to the staff, now drawn from the Community of the Resurrection and the Deaconess Community of St. Andrew. Her last visit was in June 1984.

Queen Eizabeth has a sincere and simple Christian faith which she has always practised from her earliest days. She and the King benefited by their close friendship with the late Dr. Edward Woods, Bishop of Lichfield, dating from the time the present Queen was a baby. She always attends a service of worship

every Sunday and although any visitors are not obliged to answer her summons of 'anybody coming to church', almost invariably they do so.

Her Majesty has followed her mother's advice – 'If you find anyone a bore, it's your fault', and her philosophy of life may be summed up in what she told her daughters when they were young 'Your work is the rent you pay for the room you occupy on earth.' In South Africa she was told that everyone had felt a warmth radiating from her and was asked 'Do you feel that you are giving something out?' 'I must admit', she said, 'that at times I feel something flow out of me. It makes me very tired for a moment. Then I seem to get something back from the people, sympathy, goodwill. I do not know exactly, and I feel strength again, in fact recharged. It is an exchange, I expect.'

The Queen Mother, like the Queen, Prince Philip and the Prince of Wales, issues her own Royal Warrants. Among this number are several firms of prestige who have supplied products to Her Majesty, but some are small establishments such as a cheesemonger in Orkney, a fruiterer at Thurso, a saddler at Lambourn in Berkshire, and a grocer at Castleton in Caithness. In 1984 for instance, among new warrants is that of Greenstage of Newmarket who supply Musk sausages.

Her Majesty is a Lady of the Garter and a Lady of the Thistle, the two most exclusive Orders of Chivalry in the world still conferred, and a Lady of the Crown of India. This last Order to honour ladies was established in 1877 by Queen Victoria to commemorate her title of Empress of India. King George VI made the last appointments in 1947 to his daughters the present Queen and Princess Margaret. There are only three other living ladies with this honour, Princess Alice, Duchess of Gloucester, the Maharani of Travancore and Countess Wavell.

Her other honours are Grand Master and Dame Grand Cross of the Royal Victorian Order. She is also holder of the exclusive Royal Victorian Chain and Dame Grand Cross of the British Empire and of the Order of St. John of Jerusalem. Queen Victoria founded the Royal Victorian Order in 1896 for service to the Crown and as such is highly prized. As Grand Master, the Queen Mother signs warrants of all appointments. The Chapel of the Savoy in London attached to the Order is too small to admit all members, so the last two Services were held in St. George's Chapel, Windsor.

The Queen Mother, as the last Empress of India, is keenly interested in that sub-continent. When the Indian Army Association invited her to an evening reception at St.

Opposite:
The Queen Mother and the Archbishop of Canterbury in February 1985 after the unveiling of the Lord Mountbatten Memorial.

Left:
The Queen Mother, Lady of the Garter, leaving St. George's Chapel, Windsor, with her grandson the Prince of Wales, Knight of the Garter, after the 1981 Garter Service.

Right:
As President of the
Victoria Cross and
George Cross Association,
the Queen Mother is
photographed in 1984 at
Clarence House with its
members holding V.C.s
and G.C.s.

Below:
The Queen Mother and
other members of the
Royal Family at the
Derby.

Dressed in powder blue, the Queen Mother watches the Badminton Horse Trials in 1982, founded by the late Duke of Beaufort.

James's Palace on her eighty-third birthday, she spent over two hours talking to most of the 700 guests. The President of the Association is Brigadier Hamilton, whose wife is Molly Kaye author of *The Far Pavilions*.

Every year contains many annual fixtures for the Queen Mother. She presents sprigs of shamrock to the Irish Guards on their St. Patrick's Day parade, 17th March, whether it be at Münster in West Germany, as she did in 1984, Chelsea Barracks in London or elsewhere. The first time the Guards were presented with shamrock was in 1901 by Queen Alexandra. Then during April comes the Badminton Horse Trials, in May the Chelsea Flower Show, and many appointments in June including Derby Day, Trooping the Colour on Horse Guards Parade in London on the Queen's Official Birthday, the Annual Service of the Order of the Garter in St. George's Chapel, Windsor, and the four-day Ascot Royal Meeting. In July there are the Royal Garden Parties and the King's Lynn Festival, and early in September the Braemar Games. November has the Royal British Legion's Festival of Remembrance held in the Royal Albert Hall during which thousands of poppies descend, each representing a life forfeited, and on the following day, Remembrance Sunday, the annual ser-

Above:
The Royal Ascot Meeting
of 1970. The Queen
Mother drives down the
course accompanied by
Princess Anne.

Opposite:
At a St. Patrick's Day
Parade of the Irish
Guards, the Queen
Mother admires the Irish
Wolfhound, their
regimental mascot.

vice at the Cenotaph is marked with two minutes' silence at 11.00 a.m. to remember all those killed in two World Wars and subsequent campaigns.

Though as a girl Her Majesty enjoyed riding, she did not continue. Her great passion is in steeplechasing. Her grandfather, the 13th Earl of Strathmore, was a great racehorse owner, as was his relative John Bowes, who won the Derby four times.

The Queen Mother's interest in National Hunt racing was primarily due to the late Lord Mildmay of Flete who, despite his height of 1.93m (6ft 4in), was the best-known amateur steeplechaser of his time. In the Ascot week of 1949 when he was staying with the King and Queen at Windsor Castle, the conversation turned to racing. Anthony Mildmay, known as 'Lordy' in racing circles, suggested that she would become more interested in steeplechasing if she owned a horse herself. She turned to her daughter, the present Queen, and as a result they decided to go half-shares in owning a jumper.

Major Peter Cazalet, who trained Lord Mildmay's horses, bought for them 'Monaveen' an Irish nine-year-old who raced in Princess Elizabeth's colours. During that October 'Monaveen', ridden by Tony Grantham, their first jockey, was a winner at Fontwell Park, but in the next year they suffered one of the tragedies of National Hunt racing. 'Monaveen' broke his leg at Hurst Park and had to be put down, which upset both royal owners.

Earlier in the same year Anthony Mildmay, while taking an early bathe on his private beach in Devon, tragically suffered a sudden seizure and was drowned. Major Cazalet suggested that Queen Elizabeth should buy one of his best horses, 'Manicou'. Her daughter did not continue the partnership being more interested in breeding and in flat racing, as indeed was the King. In October the Queen Mother registered as her racing colours those of her grandfather: a pale blue shirt with buff stripes, with pale blue sleeves and a black cap with gold tassels.

The Queen Mother and other members of the Royal Family attending the Braemar Games.

On Boxing Day 1950 'Manicou' won the King George VI Chase at Kempton Park. For the first time a Queen's horse had won a race under her colours since Queen Anne in 1714. Queen Elizabeth took the greatest interest in her horses. During one state visit she was dancing at Buckingham Palace until 3.00 a.m. Even so, she rose early to see her guests leave, and then drove down to Kempton to see 'Manicou' run.

One of the Queen Mother's horses, 'Gay Record', proved a difficult horse to manage. She heard of an Irish trainer, Jack O'Donoghue, living at Reigate in Surrey who had a great success with 'Trapeze' who utterly refused to climb into a horsebox. She sought him out, and went down to his cottage, taking with her the Queen, 'who had a slack afternoon'. As a result O'Donoghue performed a near miracle on 'Gay Record'. So successful was the partnership in fact that O'Donoghue received a telegram from the Queen Mother 'So delighted that it was "Gay Record" who gave me my century of wins.'

Queen Elizabeth went down to Reigate several times afterwards. 'She usually brings her three corgis with her', O'Donoghue said 'and they run about all over the place. She's often in old clothes. She always brings apples and feeds the horses.'

The Queen Mother's most famous horse was 'Devon Loch', bought shortly before the King's death. Four years later in March 1956 'Devon Loch' ran in an unforgettable Grand National, ridden by Dick Francis. The Royal Family assembled in force at Aintree to see 'Devon Loch' clear the final fence six lengths in the lead. The crowd cheered to a crescendo as he neared the winning post, for the Queen Mother is extremely popular. Suddenly 45.7m (50yds) from the post 'Devon Loch' collapsed, sprawling on all fours. The Queen Mother, aghast, said 'I must go down and comfort those poor people' and hurried to the scene. She found Major Cazalet dumbfounded with Dick Francis and the stable lads in tears. 'Ma'am everyone's all right, no one's hurt but you

Above:
The Queen Mother with Lord Mildmay and her Jockey Tony Grantham looks at her horse 'Monaveen' in the enclosure. This was her first steeplechaser.

Left:
The Queen Mother presents the Queen with a sprig of shamrock at the St. Patrick's Day Parade of the Irish Guards at Windsor in 1980. This was the first occasion that the Queen attended the Parade.

should have won', Cazalet said. She shrugged her shoulders at her own loss 'That's racing', she said, and went to see 'Devon Loch', saying 'You dear, poor old boy'.

What happened has never been satisfactorily explained. It is possible that he tried to jump the shadow cast by the water jump, or perhaps he slipped. The most logical explanation though, is that the thunderous cheers at the National frightened the horse. Her Majesty gave Major Cazalet a silver cigarette box inscribed 'A memento of that terrible and yet glorious day'. To Dick Francis she also gave a cigarette box inscribed 'Devon Loch's National', with a cheque and a note to cheer him up.

'Devon Loch' had an unexpected win at Nottingham several months later. Half way through the race the horse suddenly picked up with a burst of speed to win by two lengths. By 1957 his racing days were over and Her Majesty gave him to Noel (now Sir Noel) Murless at Newmarket, to be ridden as a hack by his daughter Julie. Lady Murless remembers the many visits the Queen Mother made to see her old horse, to whom

she was devoted. He used to nestle up to her, throwing back his ears with delight, and she always remembered to take him sugar lumps and apples. She never sells her retired horses but sees that they all have good homes. Just before 'Devon Loch' had to be put down in 1962 he returned to Sandringham.

In 1964, when Queen Elizabeth was recovering in hospital from an operation, Peter Cazalet sent her large bouquets of lilac, daffodils and tulips from 'Double Star' and 'The Rip', with rosebuds from 'Rochfort', her 'darling boys'. She wrote 'please thank them from their loving and grateful owner for this imaginative, amusing and beautiful present'.

'The Rip' became her special favourite. Bred from her own horse 'Manicou' out of 'Easy Virtue', his owner Jack Irwin, landlord of the Red Cat Inn at Wootton Marshes near Sandringham, entered him as a foal in some local shows (he was then named 'Spoilt Union'), which he invariably won. This news reached Queen Elizabeth, who went to inspect him in the paddock adjoining the Inn. When a two-year-old, he was sold to her for 400 guineas, having changed his unattractive name to 'The Rip'.

In December 1961 'The Rip' helped to secure for her a hat trick at Lingfield. Her horse 'Laffy' won the 1.30 p.m. race, 'Double Star' the second and 'The Rip' the third. Her Majesty went down to the Cazalets for a weekend of triple celebration. In all, 'The Rip' won thirteen times, but he only finished seventh in the 1965 Grand National.

Four sons of 'Queen of the Isle' provided Her Majesty with a success story. The full brothers 'Colonius' and 'Isle of Man', and their half-brother 'Inch Arran', won forty-two races between them. In fact, when 'Inch Arran' won the Topham Trophy at Aintree it proved to be the last to be trained by Peter Cazalet. Another half-brother, 'Queen's College', also won twice.

When Major Cazalet died in 1973, the Queen Mother showed her great appreciation of his own and his stables' services by giving presents to everyone: the blacksmith, the gallops man and all the stable lads. Another racing friend, Fulke Walwyn, a retired 9th Lancers officer, the doyen of National Hunt trainers, who had won the 1937 Grand National on 'Reynoldstown', succeeded as Queen Elizabeth's chief trainer.

Fulke Walwyn's first two big races for her were the Fairlawne Chase, appropriately called after Peter Cazalet's stables, won by 'Game Spirit' at Windsor and 'Sunyboy' who

The Queen Mother at Sandown Park in January 1956 to see her horse 'Devon Loch' run in the Mildmay Memorial Chase. She gives him a pat for good luck in the paddock.

In the unsaddling enclosure at Sandown Park in March 1981 Her Majesty greets her horse 'Special Cargo' after winning the Alanbrooke Memorial Handicap Chase.

won at Wolverhampton. 'Game Spirit' was a famous and popular steeplechaser who won more races for her than any other horse and never ran a bad race. He was very appropriately named. Unfortunately he dropped dead after completing the course at Newbury, where a race was later named after him. 'Sunyboy', bought from Lady Beaverbrook, came second at Cheltenham and was a first-class hurdler. In February 1976, ridden by Bill Smith, he won the Fernbank Hurdle at

Ascot to become the Queen Mother's three hundredth winner and broke the Ascot 4.80 kilometres (3 miles) record. He was later retired to stud.

Queen Elizabeth's greatest success so far came in 1975, only to be surpassed in 1984 by 'Special Cargo's' great victory. This was when 'Tammuz', ridden by Bill Smith, won the highly prized Schweppes Gold Trophy at Newbury. Although she raced this great hurdler, he was bred by the Queen.

Well wrapped up, the Queen Mother at a Sandringham shooting party in January 1981 with Maurice Melton, then under-keeper.

Without any doubt 'Special Cargo's' spectacular finish in this race has been the most exciting steeplechase anyone can remember. Ridden by Kevin Mooney, he suddenly came up from the rear at a tremendous speed to become one of four horses in the photo finish, winning in the last stride and breaking the course record. The Queen Mother was given a tremendous reception. That summer she celebrated by giving a garden party at Clarence House to all those connected with the horse.

During the 1960s Queen Elizabeth usually had about fifteen horses in training, principally with Major Cazalet. Today she has seven, all with Mr. Walwyn at Saxon House at Lambourn in Berkshire. At the time of writing she has had 352 winners.

Mr. Michael Oswald, the Queen's Stud Manager at Sandringham and Wolferton, whose wife, Lady Angela, is a lady-in-waiting to Queen Elizabeth, has looked after her horses for the last fifteen years, while Sir Martin Gilliat deals with the social side. Like the Queen, she breeds horses and takes a great interest in the Royal studs which she visits frequently when at Sandringham. The people working at both studs love to show her around, and as a result Michael Oswald, as far as is possible, equally divides her horses between the two studs so that none of the men are disappointed in not seeing her.

It has been said that Her Majesty has done more than anyone else since Lord Mildmay for National Hunt racing, but it would be wrong to think that she enjoys only steeplechasing, for she takes also a keen interest in the Queen's horses and in flat racing. She became Patron of the National Hunt Committee in 1954 and of the Injured Jockeys' Fund in 1974, with which she keeps in very close touch.

Her Majesty never bets. She regards racing purely as a sport, and keeps her purchases of horses to a sensible limit. Today she races as much as she ever did and likes nothing better than to go to Sandown, Kempton, Newbury, Ascot and Windsor, and occasionally to Cheltenham.

'She's a wonderful person to ride for', said her principal jockey Kevin Mooney, who succeeded on Bill Smith's recent retirement. The advice she gives her jockeys is proverbial. Before a race she tells them 'You know what to do, don't you? Go out and look after each other.'

The Queen Mother has had an impressive array of jockeys since her first, Tony Gran-

Coming towards the present day, 'Special Cargo', now aged twelve, started to win races in the 1978-9 season, but developed appalling leg trouble for which he had to have carbon fibre implants in the tendons of his forelegs. He made his comeback in the winter of 1983-4 and has since won four races, including the Grand Military Gold Cup at Sandown and the very prestigious Whitbread Gold Cup in April 1984, which made that year the most successful in the Queen Mother's racing.

ham, who rode 'Monaveen' and 'Manicou'. Included in the number are Dick Francis and Arthur Freeman, who nearly missed his chance to ride for her. Major Cazalet rang up to ask him if he could ride at Fontwell Park in Sussex. He was out at a Cambridge cinema at the time, when a message was flashed on the screen, 'Arthur Freeman come home'. He only drove as far as Newmarket in his brand new Sunbeam Talbot when it broke down. All he could do was to take a taxi back to Cambridge and then dash to hire a plane to fly him to Sussex. He arrived just in time.

Bill Rees first won on 'The Rip' after Freeman's retirement. He later lay four months on his back in hospital after 'Dunkirk' fell on him on Boxing Day 1965 at Kempton and was killed. In all, Rees rode fifty-one winners for Her Majesty. David Mould rode his first winner in the 1959-60 season, and later all fourteen of her winners from Fair-awne.

Though the Queen Mother gives presents to all those who work for her in racing, rarely does she arrange to be specially photographed. When her jockey, Terry Biddlecombe, rode for her for the last time she gave him a signed colour photograph of herself with him and Fulke Walwyn in the paddock at Cheltenham.

'The blower' (racing information service), was installed at Clarence House in 1965. She likes to follow the progress of her horses when unable to get to the races. In the days of Major Cazalet, the Queen Mother used to give an annual party at Clarence House for her trainers, jockeys, ex-jockeys and head lads, at which she was the only lady present. There was much talk of horses, no one enjoying these occasions more than Her Majesty.

When the Queen Mother went to the Cheltenham Races during March she would pass a grocer's store in the town. Children and elderly people gathered at Philip Delaney's shop to watch the royal car slow down on her way home at about 4.30 p.m. and wave their Union Jacks he had supplied. Once in March the car slowed down, but the time was 4.15 as the last race had been cancelled. Mr. Delaney stood alone, the rest arrived late and were disappointed.

Next year they asked him to write to Clarence House to ask the time Her Majesty would pass by. 'At 4.40,' he was told. Sure enough, in 1969 the royal car slowed down and then stopped. The Queen Mother got out, and much to Philip Delaney's delight

and surprise she shook his hand and carried on a long conversation. He had sold out of Union Jacks and gave the children wild daffodils to wave. He was holding the bulk of them, a rather ragged collection with slimy stalks. The Queen Mother asked 'Are these for me?' He apologized that they were unwrapped and not more exotic. 'Just how I like them' she said.

Every year, on her way home from the races, the Queen Mother stopped at 4.40 to see Mr. Delaney and his group of old people and children. That is, until 1981. He then told her that he was moving 4.80 kilometres (3 miles) off the route to Prestbury, and thought that this would end the custom. Her Majesty said she would still come, despite the detour, though on her way in the morning. Jasmine and wild flowers are usually given her by this group of ardent 'Queen Mum fans', with a box of her favourite mint chocolates.

The Queen Mother grew up surrounded by dogs and has never been without them. She introduced corgis with 'Dookie' in 1933

Princess Margaret and the Royal corgis welcome back the Queen Mother at Heathrow Airport after her seven weeks' tour of Australia and New Zealand in 1966.

A porter at the Central London Meat Market at Smithfield in April 1982 gives Her Majesty a warm welcome.

and has remained loyal to this breed, though some of them do have tantrums at times. At present she has a much-loved elderly corgi aged fourteen, 'Geordie', whose companion, 'Blackie', had to be put down after Christmas 1983 after losing nearly all his teeth. A young recruit, 'Kirsty', born at the beginning of 1984, has now filled 'Blackie's' place. The Queen Mother exercises her dogs personally, however wet or cold it may be outside, and likes nothing better than to take them for brisk walks.

Fly fishing is a sport in which Her Majesty excels. In the Dee, or along a neighbour's stretch of the River Thurso when she is at the Castle of Mey, she enjoys to fish for salmon. Recently she has cut down this a little and on the Queen's advice no longer wades waist deep for hours on end.

She taught the Prince of Wales fly fishing, and he is the only other expert royal angler, although Prince Edward is taking it up. In turn Prince Charles tried to teach the Princess of Wales but constantly prying cameras put her off.

The Queen Mother demonstrated that she was a skilful snooker player at a Press Club party given to her for her eightieth birthday. She enjoys crossword puzzles, and usually completes that in the *Daily Telegraph* and sometimes one other.

At Clarence House there are several traditional British Royal Family portraits, as well as French Impressionists and modern paintings that were collected by the Queen Mother. The former include two by Allan Ramsay of George III and his mother, Augusta Princess of Wales, Sir William Beechey's George III and Queen Charlotte, and John Hoppner's portraits of their sons, the Dukes of Clarence and Kent.

The Queen Mother has a Hoppner of the 10th Earl of Strathmore. It was his son John Bowes (by Mary Milner, whom he married a day before he died) who established the Bowes Museum (Her Majesty is Patron of the Friends there), but he was unsuccessful in claiming the Earldom of Strathmore. Incidentally, John Bowes owned four Derby winners, of whom one of them, 'Cotherstone'

The Queen Mother in animated conversation with nineteen-year-old Alan Skilton of Guildford. He is taking part in outdoor adventure training courses with the Operation Drake Fellowhip aboard the Thames Sailing Barge Dannebrog at St. Katharine's Dock, London 1982.

Right:
The Queen Mother came to St. Peter's Walworth in South London in 1982 for a service of rededication. Here she visits a social club in the crypt after the service.

Right:
At the opening of the Mayflower Family Centre Youth Club London, in March 1980, the Queen Mother showed her skill at the snooker table. 'Cor, I wish I could play as well as that' said one boy.

appears in a picture by John Herring. Another Herring shows the 12th Earl of Strathmore in his racing colours. There is a delightful picture by Sir William Richmond of the three young Misses Cavendish-Bentinck, one of whom became Lady Strathmore, Queen Elizabeth's mother.

Hanging in the Lower Corridor is a study of King George VI by Simon Elwes for his large painting 'The Investiture of Princess Elizabeth with the Order of the Garter by King George VI'. John Singer Sargent portrays the Queen in the year of her wedding, and two de Laszlos, of her with the King, and Terence Cuneo's study of her in Coronation Robes.

Augustus John is represented by the head of George Bernard Shaw, entitled 'When Homer Nods, or the Philosopher in Contemplation' (Shaw's eyes are shut), and his uncompleted painting of the Queen Mother. According to Michael Holroyd, when he was approached to paint Her Majesty he was appalled to hear that he must always appear dead sober, and asked if he must appear dead sober when he left. The portrait was left unfinished as Augustus John often did not turn up on appointed days, and had to be enticed with a bottle of brandy at Buckingham Palace, kept in the cupboard with his brushes. After the Palace was bombed, Her Majesty offered to sit in his studio as there were no windows but it was no good; he had abandoned the work. When he died in 1961 a dealer found the uncompleted picture in a cellar drawer and presented it to the Queen Mother.

Among the many modern works by British painters she has collected are Wilson Steer, Sir William Nicholson, Duncan Grant, Dame Ethel Walker, Paul Nash and Edward Seago. Sidney Nolan, from Australia, is represented by 'Strange Fruit' and L.S. Lowry's 'Fylde Farm', is dated 1943, before he turned to industrial scenes with matchstick figures.

The Queen Mother has a fine display of silver such as the superb dessert service made in 1787 for Queen Charlotte and also part of Queen Mary's Collection. The splendid dinner service of Worcester was presented by George IV to the King of Hanover. When racing friends are entertained, silver cups are often displayed including the replica of the famous Lanark Bell won in 1946 by the King's horse 'Kingstone'. Catalogues of the main salerooms are carefully studied to see when any pictures, silver or furniture of family interest are being offered for sale.

Some of these treasures were shown in Richard Cawston's television film *Royal Heritage* in 1977. The Queen Mother appeared on the final programme of this series with Sir Huw Wheldon. She talked about the bombing of Buckingham Palace, her finding and buying the Castle of Mey and her collection of pictures. It seems incongruous that whereas she is so noted for putting people at ease in real life, she should seldom appear on televsion, especially as her part in the programme was considered to be the best of the series.

From her earliest days the Queen Mother has been a keen gardener, from the time when she had her own little plot edged with thyme. She prefers the natural English style to the formal French garden. On being asked to name her favourite flower, she invariably answers 'I like *all* flowers.' Even so it seems

Portrait of the 12th Earl of Strathmore in his racing colours by John Frederick Herring, from the Queen Mother's collection.

that the sweet scent of roses, pastel-coloured sweet peas and lilies of the valley with their lovely aroma do give her real pleasure.

As Queen, she became the owner of many gardens, including Buckingham Palace, Windsor Castle, Balmoral and Sandringham, but it was the gardens of Royal Lodge which owe so much to her late husband and herself. They must have planted thousands of spring bulbs and busily worked in clearing, designing and planting the gardens from scratch. The gardens at Birkhall, too, were planted by them both and included cornflowers, larkspur and Michaelmas daisies.

The gardens of the Castle of Mey proved the greatest challenge. After years of neglect, the Queen Mother restored them to their full beauty. In the walled garden the old hedges remain containing such shrubs as hardy fuchsia, wild dog-rose and flowering currant, which divides the area into a series of protected squares. Beyond a fence swathed in honeysuckle she has created a little rose

garden. Between the west front of the Castle and the walled garden is a lawn surrounded by roses, a favourite spot to take meals out of doors.

Today the Queen Mother leaves heavy work to the gardeners, but enjoys her gardens as much as ever. The beautiful pink 'Elizabeth of Glamis' roses, introduced at the 1964 Chelsea Flower Show, were named in her honour by the growers, Samuel McGredy & Son of Northern Ireland.

The London Gardens Society, founded in 1934, by Lord Noel Buxton to encourage Londoners to grow flowers in their small gardens or even in window boxes, is one of the Patronages of the Queen Mother. She enjoys visiting these gardens when she takes tea alone with one family. One year the organizer asked if she would be willing to visit an extra garden and forego her cup of tea. Back came the reply that she loved her tea but she would visit the *extra* garden in *addition* to the schedule.

A retired Merchant Navy man, whom she met on visiting his garden, mentioned that he hoped that Her Majesty would have a happy day on 4th August as this also happened to be his own birthday. When that day came she sent him a telegram of best wishes.

The Queen Mother much admired the Crazy Gang as did the King. Bud Flanagan was a great favourite with his songs, such as 'We're going to Hang out our Washing on the Siegfried Line', 'Run, Rabbit, Run', and 'Underneath the Arches'. He and Chesney Allen formed a double act, but when Allen had to retire in 1945 Flanagan turned solo. Before officially retiring in 1962, Bud Flanagan, in effect 'the King's Jester', had taken part in fifteen Royal Variety performances and gatecrashed some others. He died in 1968. The Queen Mother met Chesney Allen, last surviving member of the Crazy Gang, in March 1982 at a performance of 'Underneath the Arches' at the Prince of Wales Theatre, a few months before he died.

An actor who is grateful to Her Majesty is Tommy Steele, who made his debut in 1956 in a Royal Variety show at the Palladium. He was then England's rock'n'roll king and had just gone over to a new style that had not then met with public approval. As the audience did not react favourably to him there might well have been a disaster, had not the Queen Mother been in the Royal box. She leaned forward so that everyone could see her and started to applaud and they all followed suit!

The Royal Variety Performance of 1978 was dedicated to her and she was asked to choose her favourite performers for the occasion. However, she preferred just to drop a few hints. At the top of the bill was Gracie Fields, then aged eighty-one, who had been to Buckingham Palace earlier in the year to receive from the Queen Mother's hand the honour of Dame of the British Empire.

Gracie rehearsed and rehearsed. 'I don't want to sound like an old lady', she said. She sang her legendary 'Sally' with all the richness of her experience until she suddenly broke off near the end with great emotion, which brought her a standing ovation. She died in the following year.

Also in the caste of that Royal Variety Performance was Arthur Askey, of the same vintage as the Queen Mother. She told him 'I really shouldn't say it but this was the best Royal Variety I have ever seen'. Prince Charles later told Arthur 'You go with the century like my grandmother. That must have been a very good year'.

One of the writers the Queen Mother admires is P.G. Wodehouse. When he received his knighthood at the age of ninety-three in the 1975 New Year's Honours List marking the end of a long campaign of unjustified criticism dating from the war, she offered to go herself to the United States to confer the accolade. Alas, this knighthood came too late. Within the next two months, 'Plum' died of a heart attack. Her Majesty went on an unscheduled visit in April 1982 to the Wodehouse Exhibition, which was held in the Lyttelton Theatre on the South Bank to mark his centenary.

Dick Francis, formerly the Queen Mother's famous jockey, turned to writing racing novels, which he invariably sends to her. She particularly enjoys reading biographies and autobiographies and those she likes she recommends or passes to Princess Margaret. A particular pleasure for her was listening to Lord David Cecil reading the novels of Jane Austen on whom he is a great authority.

One of the sorrows of being an octogenarian is in outliving close friends who were near contemporaries, and so it has been with the Queen Mother. Included in this number were Sir Osbert Sitwell the writer, Sir Kenneth Clark (Lord Clark) the celebrated art historian, Tom Goff who revived interest in harpsichords and was their greatest exponent, Celia Johnson the actress and Sir John Betjeman the Poet Laureate. At Royal Lodge on occasions, Sir John recited his poems to her after dinner and accompanied her on expeditions to look over old churches, sometimes with Sir Kenneth Clark.

Today her circle of friends includes the Earl of Drogheda, former Chairman of the Royal Opera House, Lord David Cecil the historian and writer, Sir Frederick Ashton of ballet fame, with whom she delights in having conversations in French and Sir Hugh Casson, until recently President of the Royal Academy.

The Queen Mother does not mind if the younger members of the Royal Family drop in to see her at Clarence House informally dressed with open-neck shirts and jeans. Lord Snowdon started this trend by wearing polo neck jerseys. She delights in children, those of her family and all others she comes across. When a six-year-old boy was presented to her at a county agricultural show he said excitedly 'Oh Ma'am, I've met your daughter. Do you know, she's *the Queen*'. 'Yes I know', she answered. '*Isn't it* exciting!'

Her Majesty is the most popular member of the Royal Family with press photographers, and goes out of her way to pose for them. 'She's always smiling and knows exactly where to stop for us to get the best pictures,' one added. This is not to say that she condoned in any way the few unscrupulous camera men who caused such distress to the future Princess of Wales. She never forgets to thank everyone for the smallest service, such as chauffeurs, cooks in friends' houses, and shop assistants. The racing fraternity are always delighted to see her standard flying at meetings. 'Good,' they say, 'she's here.'

When the Queen Mother wishes to give a large party, which happens only occasionally, the Queen lends her some of her Buckingham Palace staff. So popular is she that they all want to go! Accordingly a roster is kept. Only a comparatively small staff is kept at Clarence House.

Some of the senior members of the Queen Mother's Household are on duty only on important and ceremonial occasions. These are her Lord Chamberlain, the Earl of Dalhousie, her Mistress of the Robes, the Dowager Duchess of Abercorn and her two senior ladies-in-waiting, the Dowager Viscountess Hambleden and Lady Grimthorpe, who are technically her Ladies of the Bedchamber.

Her Majesty has four ladies-in-waiting, officially Women of the Bedchamber, Ruth

Lady Fermoy, Mrs. Patrick Campbell-Preston, Lady Elizabeth Basset and Lady Angela Oswald, who each take a tour of duty for two weeks when they live in. In addition there is an Extra Woman of the Bedchamber, Lady Jean Rankin, who takes occasional duties. The lady-in-waiting on duty is Queen Elizabeth's constant companion. She accompanies her when she goes out, writes and answers her letters, goes shopping and generally assists to make her life easier.

The most important member of the Queen Mother's Household is her Private Secretary, Lieutenant-Colonel Sir Martin Gilliat, who arranges her programme, deals with her main correspondence and generally oversees her Household. Her treasurer, Sir Ralph Anstruther, looks after matters concerning expenses, all aspects of economy and her many Patronages. Day-to-day administration, not only of Clarence House, but also when she is in residence at Royal Lodge, Birkhall and the Castle Mey, falls to her Comptroller of the Household, Major Sir Alastair Aird, who sends out her invitations to private parties, which he runs. Her Press Secretary, Major John Griffin, deals with the media. All are devoted to the Queen Mother. A lady-in-waiting once said 'it has not only been a privilege to serve her but such fun to be with her'.

Wullie Savage, a taxi driver from Kirriemuir, once said that 'one of the best presents that Buckingham Palace ever had came from Glamis'. The Queen Mother's eventful life has not always been easy but she is an extremely happy person who enjoys being busy and fulfilling her many engagements. May she have a happy eighty-fifth birthday in 1985 with many more to come.

At a special Royal Variety performance for the Queen Mother's eightieth birthday, Her Majesty meets Mary Martin, her son Larry Hagman, otherwise J.R. Ewing, and Bruce Forsyth, backstage at the London Palladium.

187

Bibliography

Works consulted:

Asquith, Lady Cynthia	*Queen Elizabeth* 1937
Buckle, Richard (editor)	*Self Portrait with Friends. The Selected Diaries of Cecil Beaton 1926–1974*
Cathcart, Helen	*The Queen Herself* 1982
	The Queen Mother Herself 1979
Chandos, Lord	*The Memoirs of Lord Chandos* 1962
Day, James Wentworth	*The Queen Mother's Family History* 1979
Donaldson, Frances	*Edward VIII* 1974
Duff, David	*Elizabeth of Glamis* 1980
	George and Elizabeth 1983
	Mother of the Queen 1965
Ellis, Jennifer	*Elizabeth the Queen Mother* 1953
(editor)	*Thatched with Gold, The Memoirs of Mabel, Countess of Airlie* 1962
Glenton, William	*Tony's Room* 1965
Herbert, Ivor	*The Queen Mother's Horses* 1967
Howard, Philip	*The British Monarchy* 1977
James, Robert Rhodes (editor)	*Chips, the Diaries of Sir Henry Channon* 1967
Judd, Dennis	*King George VI* 1982
Lacey, Robert	*Majesty* 1977
Laird, Dorothy	*How the Queen Reigns* 1959
	Queen Elizabeth the Queen Mother 1975
Lane, Peter	*The Queen Mother* 1979
Liversidge, Douglas	*The Queen Mother* 1980
Longford, Elizabeth	*Elizabeth R* 1983
	The Queen Mother 1981
	The Royal House of Windsor 1974
Marie Louise, H.H. Princess	*My Memories of Six Reigns* 1947
Montague-Smith, Patrick	*The Country Life Book of the Silver Jubilee* 1976
with Montgomery-Massingberd, Hugh	*Royal Palaces, Gardens and Homes* 1981
Morrah, Dermot	*The Royal Family in Africa* 1947
	The Work of the Queen 1958
Morrow, Ann	*The Queen Mother* 1984
Nicolson, Harold	*Diaries and Letters 1930–62, 1967*
	King George V, His Life and Reign 1952
Patience, Sally	*The Queen Mother* 1977
Payn, Graham and Morley, Sheridan (editor)	*The Nöel Coward Diaries* 1982
Pope-Hennessy, James	*Queen Mary* 1959
Rose, Kenneth	*King George V* 1983
Sinclair, David	*Queen and Country* 1980
Stirton, the Rev. John, D.D.	*Glamis Castle* 1938
Talbot, Godfrey	*The Country Life Book of Queen Elizabeth the Queen Mother* 1983
	The Country Life Book of the Royal Family 1980
Thomas, Sir Miles	*Out on a Wing* 1964
Wakeford, Geoffrey	*Thirty Years a Queen* 1968
Walker, Eric Sherbrooke	*Treetops Hotel* 1962
Wheeler-Bennett, John W.	*King George VI, His Life and Reign* 1958
Whiting, Audrey	*Family Royal* 1982
Windsor, H.R.H., The Duke of	*A King's Story* 1951
Wulff, Louis	*Queen of Tomorrow* 1948
	Silver Wedding 1948
Anon.	*Royal Family in Wartime* 1945
Periodicals	Berkswell's *The Royal Year*, since 1974
	Majesty, The monthly Review, since 1980

Index

Photographic acknowledgments

BBC Hulton Picture Library, London 16, 22, 27, 28, 39, 43 right, 45 top, 46, 59, 60, 62, 64, 79, 91, 92, 104, 107, 119, 139, 142, 145 top, 146 bottom, 147, 172, 176; John Bethell Photography, St Albans, Hertfordshire 24–5; Reproduced by kind permission of The Honourable Lady Rachel Bowes Lyon 21; Bridgeman Art Library, from the Guildhall, London 75, 131; Camera Press, London 133, 140 top, 171, 173, photograph Bassano 96, Baron 100, Cecil Beaton 129, Norman Parkinson 148–9, 149, Snowdon 7, 164–5; copyright reserved to Queen Elizabeth II 17, 37, 73, 102, 183; Country Life, London 9 bottom; Daily Telegraph Colour Library, London 9 top; Mary Evans Picture Library, London 72; Tim Graham, London 70–1, 163; Illustrated London News, London 40, 51, 68, 69; Mansell Collection, London 18, 26, 47, 86 top and bottom; National Portrait Gallery, London, from the Weidenfeld Library 10, 13; Photo Source, London 23, 25, 32, 52, 53, 55, 57, 62–3, 65, 80–1, 84, 85, 87, 88, 93, 94, 97, 101 top, 105, 110, 113, 114, 115 top, 121 top, 126, 128 top, 128 bottom, 130, 134, 135, 136 top, 136 bottom, 141, 143, 144 top, 146 top, 152 bottom, 154 top, 155, 157 top, 157 bottom, 158, 160, 161, 166, 169, 170 top, 170 bottom, 174, 182 top, 182 bottom, 184, 185; Popperfoto, London 74, 83, 89, 95, 98, 101 bottom, 112, 117, 156, 175 top; Reproduced by kind permission of Her Majesty Queen Elizabeth, the Queen Mother, Clarence House 102; Royal Archives, Windsor 61; Syndication International, London 12 top, 14, 33, 36 bottom, 38, 42–3 44 top, 49, 90, 121 bottom, 122, 127, 137, 138, 140 bottom 149 bottom, 150, 151 bottom, 152 top, 159, 162, 167, 168 175 bottom, 179; John Topham Photograph Library London 11, 12 bottom, 15, 19, 20, 24, 29, 31, 34, 35, 36 top, 41, 58, 66, 77, 82, 99, 109, 115 bottom, 116, 118, 120 123, 125, 144 bottom, 145 bottom, 151 top, 153, 154 bottom, 177, 178, 180, 181, 187; Weidenfeld and Nicolson London from *Country House Camera*, C. Sykes, 44–5

Front cover: The famous smile. Her Majesty Queen Elizabeth The Queen Mother, now a vivacious eighty-five (The Photo Source, London)

Back cover: The Queen Mother with Admiral Paul Greening, Flag Officer Royal Yachts, takes a memorable trip in a gondola during her visit to Venice in October, 1984 (Tim Graham, London)

Frontispiece: A seventy-fifth birthday photograph of the Queen Mother at Clarence House by Norman Parkinson. She wears a brocade dress with a pearl and diamond brooch (Camera Press London)